# Attitudes in Rat Behaviour The

*By the same author*

When Time Is at a Premium: Cognitive-Behavioural Approaches to Single-Session Therapy and Very Brief Coaching

# Attitudes in Rational Emotive Behaviour Therapy (REBT):

## *Components, Characteristics and Adversity-related Consequences*

## Windy Dryden, Ph.D

Rationality Publications

Rationality Publications
136 Montagu Mansions, London W1U 6LQ
www.rationalitypublications.com
info@rationalitypublications.com

First edition published by Rationality Publications
Copyright (c) 2016 Windy Dryden

A catalogue record of this book is
available from the British Library.

First edition 2016

ISBN: 978-1-910301-36-4

Printed and bound in Great Britain by
Lightning Source UK Ltd,
Chapter House, Pitfield, Kiln Farm,
Milton Keynes MK11 3LW

# Contents

*This book is dedicated to the ongoing work of the Albert Ellis Institute in New York and its affiliated training centres throughout the world*

# Preface

This book is a theoretical exposition on the role that attitudes play in Rational Emotive Behaviour Therapy (REBT). I begin the book with a brief statement of what REBT is. I then make the case for using the term 'attitude' rather than the term 'belief' in REBT, before discussing the component structure and characteristic features of what were formerly known as irrational beliefs and rational beliefs in Rational Emotive Behaviour Therapy (REBT), but what I am calling here rigid and extreme attitudes and flexible and non-extreme attitudes respectively.

Basically and fundamentally, the REBT model holds that rigid and extreme attitudes are at the core of emotional problems, and flexible and non-extreme attitudes are at the core of the solutions to these problems. I conclude the book by considering the adversity-related consequences of holding both sets of attitudes. It is my hope that this exposition will help both REBT and non-REBT therapists to be clear about some important distinctive theoretical features of this pioneering approach within the cognitive-behavioural tradition of the psychological therapies.

I want to thank Richard Bennett, Demetris Katsikis and Walter Matweychuk for their valuable comments on a previous draft of this book.

I also want to thank Sage Publications for allowing me to use some of the material that appears in Chapter 1.

*Windy Dryden*
*July 2016*
*London and Eastbourne*

# 1

# What is Rational Emotive Behaviour Therapy?

## 1.1   Overview and Key Points

Rational emotive behaviour therapy (REBT) is a distinctive approach within the cognitive-behavioural tradition of psychotherapy that was developed by Albert Ellis (1913–2007). It is generally regarded as the first CBT approach and has recently celebrated its 60th birthday. Some of its key points are as follows:

- REBT emphasises the interdependence of cognition, emotion and behaviour.
- It argues that rigid and extreme attitudes[1] are at the core of psychologically disturbed responses to adversity, and flexible and non-extreme attitudes are at the core of psychologically healthy responses to the same adversity.
- It follows that a central task of REBT therapists is to encourage clients to develop flexible and non-extreme attitudes towards adversity.
- In carrying out this central task, effective REBT therapists need to be good therapists, good

---

[1] In general, in REBT theory, what I call attitudes are known as beliefs. In this book, I discuss this use of nomenclature in Chapter 2.

psychological educators and tend to practise in their own lives what they 'preach' in the consulting room.

- Meaningful psychological change is deemed to be difficult and clients need to commit themselves to an ongoing routine of thinking flexibly and in non-extreme ways in the face of adversity and of taking action that supports and reinforces such thinking. Therapists need to help clients to make this commitment in the first place and to renew this commitment during the therapeutic process and beyond

## 1.2    Brief History

Rational emotive behaviour therapy (REBT) was founded in 1955 by Albert Ellis, an American clinical psychologist who had become increasingly disaffected with psychoanalysis in which he trained in the late 1940s. Originally the approach was called rational therapy (RT) because Ellis wanted to emphasise its rational and cognitive features. In doing so, Ellis demonstrated the philosophical influences (largely Stoic) on his thinking. In 1961 he changed its name to rational-emotive therapy to show critics that it did not neglect emotions, and over thirty years later, in 1993, Ellis renamed the approach yet again, calling it rational emotive behaviour therapy to show critics that it did not neglect behaviour.

In the early 1960s Ellis (1962) published *Reason and Emotion in Psychotherapy*, a collection largely of previously published papers or previously delivered lectures, but which became a seminal work in the history of psychotherapy and which was revised 32 years later (Ellis, 1994). Most of REBT's major present-day features are described in this book: the pivotal role of cognition in psychological disturbance; the principle of psychological interactionism where cognition, emotion and behaviour are seen as interacting, not separate, systems; the advantages of self-acceptance over self-esteem in helping clients with their disturbed views of their selves; and the importance of an active-directive therapeutic style, to name but a few.

Albert Ellis died in 2007 after an unfortunate period during which he was in dispute on a number of issues with the institute that continues to bear his name. Despite this, the legacy that Ellis left REBT and the wider field of psychotherapy is untarnished and unquestioned.

REBT is practised all over the world and has many different therapeutic, occupational, coaching and educational applications. However, it tends to live in the shadow of Aaron Beck's cognitive therapy, an approach to cognitive-behaviour therapy which has attracted a greater number of practitioners and is more academically respectable.

## 1.3    Basic Assumptions

Here I will discuss: (a) the concept of rationality; (b) REBT's ABC framework; and (c) REBT's view of human nature.

### 1.3.1   Rationality

Rationality is a concept that is normally applied to a person's attitudes. So-called 'rational' attitudes, which are deemed to be at the core of psychological health, are flexible or non-extreme, consistent with reality, logical, and both self- and relationship-enhancing.[2] So-called 'irrational' attitudes, which are deemed to be at the core of psychological disturbance, are rigid or extreme, inconsistent with reality, illogical, and both self- and relationship-defeating.

### 1.3.1.1 *Four Types of Rational Attitudes*

There are four types of 'rational'[3] attitudes: flexible attitudes ('I want to be approved, but I don't have to be'); non-awfulising attitudes ('It's bad to be disapproved, but it isn't the end of the world'); discomfort tolerance attitudes ('It is difficult to face being disapproved, but I can tolerate it and it is worth it to me to do so. I am willing to tolerate it and I am going to do so'); and acceptance attitudes (e.g. self-acceptance, 'Being disapproved is bad, but it does not make me a bad person. I can accept myself as a fallible human being if I am disapproved'; other acceptance, 'It is bad if you disapprove of me, but you are not a bad person if you do so. You are a fallible human being for acting badly'; and life acceptance, 'Even though this tragedy happened which is very bad, life is not all bad. I can accept life for its complexity as it comprises good, bad and neutral events').

### 1.3.1.2 *Four Types of Irrational Attitudes*

Similarly, there are four types of 'irrational' attitudes which I present here in their condensed form: rigid attitudes ('I must be approved'); awfulising attitudes ('If I'm disapproved, it's the end of the world'); discomfort intolerance attitudes ('I can't tolerate being disapproved'); and depreciation attitudes

---

[2] I will expand on this in Chapter 3.
[3] Henceforth in this book, I will refer to 'rational' attitudes as flexible and non-extreme and 'irrational' attitudes as rigid and extreme.

(e.g. self-depreciation, 'I am worthless if I am disapproved'; other depreciation, 'You are horrible if you disapprove of me'; and life depreciation, 'Life is all bad because this tragedy happened').

### 1.3.2 The ABC Framework

REBT advocates a situational 'ABC' model of psychological disturbance and health. 'A' stands for Adversity, which occurs within a situation and can be actual or inferred. 'A' represents the aspect of the situation that the person focuses on and evaluates. 'B' stands for the Basic attitudes ('flexible and non-extreme' or 'rigid and extreme') on which 'C' rests. 'C' stands for the Consequences of holding an attitude towards A and can be emotional, behavioural and cognitive. Thus, 'As' do not cause 'Cs' but contribute to them. 'Bs' are seen as the prime but not the only determinants of 'Cs'.

Holding flexible and non-extreme attitudes towards an 'A' leads to healthy emotions, functional behaviour, and realistic and balanced subsequent thinking. Holding rigid and extreme attitudes towards the same 'A' leads to unhealthy emotions, dysfunctional behaviour, and unrealistic subsequent thinking that is highly skewed to the negative. I will discuss this issue in greater detail in Chapter 5 but see Table 1.1 for a summary.

### 1.3.3 REBT's View of Human Nature

REBT's view of human nature is realistic. Humans are seen as having the potential for both flexible and non-extreme thinking and rigid and extreme thinking. The ease with which we transform our strong desires into rigid demands suggests that the tendency towards rigid thinking is biologically based, but can be buffered or encouraged by environmental contexts.

**Table 1.1**  REBT's situational ABC framework

| Situation | |
| --- | --- |
| A = Adversity | |
| **B = Basic attitudes**<br>• Rigid and extreme attitudes | **B = Basic attitudes**<br>• Flexible and non-extreme attitudes |
| **C = Consequences**<br>• Unhealthy negative emotions<br>• Dysfunctional behaviour<br>• Unrealistic and highly negative subsequent thinking | **C = Consequences**<br>• Healthy negative emotions<br>• Functional behaviour<br>• Realistic and balanced subsequent thinking |

Clients often have the unfortunate experience of inheriting tendencies towards disturbance and being exposed to their parents' disturbed behaviour. REBT is optimistic and realistic here. It argues that if such clients work persistently and forcefully to counter their rigid and extreme attitudes and act in ways that are consistent with their flexible and non-extreme attitudes, then they can help themselves significantly. However, REBT also acknowledges that most clients will not put in this degree of effort over a long period of time and will therefore fall far short of achieving their potential for psychological health.

## 1.4    Origin and Maintenance of Problems

People are disturbed not by events but by the rigid and extreme attitudes that they take towards them. This means that while negative events contribute to the development of disturbance, particularly when these events are highly aversive, disturbance occurs when people bring their tendencies to hold rigid attitudes towards these events.

### 1.4.1    REBT's View on the Origins of Problems

REBT does not have an elaborate view on the origin of disturbance. Having said this, it does acknowledge that it is very easy for humans when they are young to disturb themselves about highly aversive events. However, it argues that even under these conditions people react differently to the same event and thus we need to understand what a person brings to and takes from a negative activating event. People learn their standards and goals from their culture, but disturbance occurs when they bring their rigid and extreme attitudes to circumstances where their standards are not met and their pursuit of their goals is blocked.

### 1.4.2    REBT's View on the Maintenance of Problems

REBT has a more elaborate view of how disturbance is maintained. It argues that people perpetuate their disturbance for a number of reasons including the following:

- They lack the insight that their disturbance is underpinned by their rigid and extreme attitudes and think instead that it is caused by events.

- They wrongly think that once they understand that their problems are underpinned by rigid and extreme attitudes, this understanding alone will lead to change.
- They do not work persistently to change their rigid and extreme attitudes and to integrate the flexible and non-extreme alternatives to these attitudes into their attitudinal system.
- They continue to act in ways that are consistent with their rigid and extreme attitudes.
- They lack or are deficient in important social skills, communication skills, problem-solving skills and other life skills.
- They think that their disturbance has payoffs that outweigh the advantages of the healthy alternatives to their disturbed feelings and/or behaviour.
- They live in environments which support the rigid and extreme attitudes that underpin their problems and they think that as this is the case they cannot do anything to help themselves.

## 1.5    Theory of Change

REBT therapists consider that the core facilitative conditions of empathy, unconditional acceptance and genuineness are often desirable, but neither necessary nor sufficient for constructive therapeutic change (Ellis, 1959). For such change to take place, REBT therapists need to help their clients to do the following:

- realise that they largely create their own psychological problems and that while situations contribute to these problems, they are in general of lesser importance in the change process;
- fully recognise that they are able to address and overcome these problems;
- understand that their problems stem largely from rigid and extreme attitudes;
- detect their rigid and extreme attitudes and discriminate between them and their flexible and non-extreme attitudes;
- question their rigid and extreme attitudes and their flexible and non-extreme attitudes until they see clearly that the former are false, illogical and unconstructive while the latter are true, sensible and constructive;
- work towards the internalisation of their new flexible and non-extreme attitudes by using a variety of cognitive (including imaginal), emotive and behavioural change methods;
- refrain from acting in ways that are consistent with their old rigid and extreme attitudes;
- extend this process of challenging attitudes and using multimodal methods of change into other areas of their lives and to commit to doing so for as long as necessary.

### 1.5.1   The Working Alliance in REBT

All this is best done when effective REBT therapists develop, maintain and suitably end a good working alliance with clients (Dryden, 2009). This involves:

- therapists and clients having a good working bond;
- therapists and clients sharing a common view of the determinants of the latter's problems and how these can best be addressed;
- therapists and clients working towards agreed goals;
- therapists and clients executing agreed tasks designed to facilitate goal achievement.

## 1.6    Skills and Strategies

In this section I will outline a number of key skills and strategies of REBT and illustrate these with a case example.

### 1.6.1  Teaching the ABC Framework and Seeking Informed Consent

REBT therapists see themselves as good psychological educators and therefore seek to teach their clients the ABC model of understanding and dealing with their psychological problems. They stress that there are alternative ways of addressing these problems and strive to elicit from their clients informed consent at the outset and throughout the therapeutic process. If they think that a client is better suited to a different approach to therapy, they do not hesitate to effect a suitable referral.

#### 1.6.1.1 *Case Example*

*Marie sought help from me for her public speaking anxiety. After hearing about the nature of anxiety, I outlined an ABC perspective on her problem and sought informed consent to proceed from Marie which she gave.*

## 1.6.2   Style and Focus

REBT therapists frequently employ an active-directive therapeutic style and use both Socratic and didactic teaching methods. However, they vary their style from client to client. They begin by working with specific examples of identified client problems and help their clients to set healthy goals. They employ a sequence of steps in working on these examples which involves using the situationally based ABC framework, questioning attitudes and negotiating suitable homework assignments with their clients.

### 1.6.2.1 *Case Example*

*I helped Marie to see that she was anxious about her mind going blank and thinking that this meant that was revealing her personal inadequacy. She also thought that people would invariably think negatively about her if this happened. I encouraged her to assume temporarily that her mind would go blank and that people would judge her negatively and encouraged her to question that this was evidence for personal inadequacy. As a result of my questioning, Marie came to see that going blank was evidence of human fallibility and not personal inadequacy as was being judged negatively by others. She undertook to speak publically at every opportunity in order to practise this new philosophy.*

## 1.6.3   Helping Client to Generalise and Deal with Core Attitudes

Helping clients to generalise their learning from situation to situation is explicitly built into the therapeutic process. So too is helping clients to identify, challenge and change core rigid and extreme attitudes which are seen as accounting for disturbance across a broad range of relevant situations.

### 1.6.3.1 *Case Example*

*I also helped Marie to practise this self-accepting attitude in other relevant contexts, such as meeting new people socially and when going on dates.*

### 1.6.4   Helping Clients to Become Their Own Therapists

A major therapeutic strategy involves helping clients to become their own therapists. In doing this, REBT therapists teach their clients how to use a particular skill such as (a) questioning rigid and extreme attitudes, (b) model the use of this skill, and sometimes (c) give the clients written instructions on how to use the skill on their own. Constructive feedback is given to encourage the refinement of the skill. As clients learn how to use the skills of REBT for themselves, their therapists adopt a less active-directive, more prompting therapeutic style in order to encourage them to take increasing responsibility for their own therapeutic change.

### 1.6.5   Flexibility

REBT may be seen as a flexible approach to counselling and psychotherapy in two main ways. First, it is an example of theoretically consistent eclecticism in that its practitioners draw upon procedures that originate from other therapeutic approaches, but do so for purposes that are consistent with REBT theory (Ellis, 2004). REBT therapists are judiciously selective in their eclecticism and avoid the use of methods that are inefficient, or mystical, or of dubious validity.

Second, while REBT therapists have their preferred therapeutic goals for their clients, namely to help them to change their core rigid and extreme attitudes and to develop and internalise a set of core flexible and non-extreme attitudes, they are, however, ready to make *compromises* with their clients on these objectives when it becomes clear that their clients are unable or unwilling to change their core rigid and extreme attitudes. In such cases, REBT therapists help their clients by encouraging them to change their distorted inferences, to effect behavioural changes or to remove themselves from negative activating events without changing their rigid and extreme attitudes.

### 1.6.5.1 *Case Example*

*Once Marie had made progress in developing her self-accepting attitude, I helped her to stand back and question her inference that others would invariably judge her negatively if her mind did go blank when giving a public presentation and for other public displays of what she judged as a weakness. Marie concluded that not everybody would judge her negatively: some would do so, others would not notice and yet others would empathise with her. Also, Marie questioned that such displays were signs of weakness. Rather, she concluded they were signs of fallibility.*

## 1.7    Research Evidence

There is quite a lot of research indicating that psychological disturbance is correlated with rigid and extreme attitudes (Vîslă, Flückiger, Holtforth and David, 2016). For example, awfulising attitudes are involved in both anxiety and pain and self-depreciation attitudes are a fundamental component of depressed mood (see Dryden, David and Ellis, 2010).

Two rigorous meta-analyses have shown REBT's effectiveness with a range of clinical and non-clinical problems (Engels, Garnefsky and Diekstra, 1993 and Lyons and Woods, 1991), although the quality of much of this research could have been improved. Well-controlled trials of REBT need to be done with clinical populations, employing well-trained REBT therapists who can be shown to adhere to a properly designed REBT competency scale (Dryden, Beal, Jones and Trower, 2010). Finally Dan David's (2015) research consistently shows that REBT does as well as other CBT approaches in comparative outcome studies.

# 2

# Attitudes Rather than Beliefs

## 2.1 Introduction

Traditionally in REBT, the term 'belief' has been used to describe a particular kind of cognitive processing that mediates between an event (either an actual event or one that is inferential in nature) or an ongoing problematic situation (such as ongoing unemployment) and the person's responses to that event or ongoing situation. While there are problems with the term 'belief', it has been retained, in part because it begins with the letter 'B' and thus shows in REBT's ABC framework that adversities at 'A' have their impact on a range of psychological responses to these adversities largely because of the 'beliefs' that people hold at 'B'.

Research that I recently carried out on how REBT's 'ABC' framework is understood by different professional and lay groups[4] revealed a large range of confusions and errors made by these groups about each element in the framework (Dryden, 2013). Some of these confusions and errors about 'B' may be cleared up by the using the term 'attitude' rather than belief since the term 'belief' is often used by people in a way that is very different from the way it is used in REBT.

---

[4] The four groups were: (a) authors of textbooks on counselling and psychotherapy; (b) REBT therapists; (c) Albert Ellis (when he was in the twilight of his career) and his wife Debbie Joffe Ellis (2011); and (d) patients in a psychiatric hospital who were taught the REBT framework.

Thus, the term 'belief' has been defined by the *Oxford Dictionary of Psychology*, 4th edition (Colman, 2015) as 'any proposition that is accepted as true on the basis of inconclusive evidence'. Thus, a client may say something like: 'I believe my boss criticised me' and while they think that they have articulated a belief, this is not actually a belief as the term has been used in REBT, but rather an inference (see Chapter 5). As we shall see, it is very important to distinguish between an inference at 'A' and an attitude (or belief in the REBT sense) at 'B' and anything that helps this distinction to be made routinely is to be welcomed. Using the term 'attitude' rather than 'belief' in REBT is one way of doing so.

Definitions of the term 'attitude' are closer to the meaning that REBT theorists ascribe to the term 'belief'. Here are three such definitions of the term 'attitude':

- 'an enduring pattern of evaluative responses towards a person, object, or issue' (Colman, 2015);

- 'a relatively enduring organization of beliefs, feelings, and behavioral tendencies towards socially significant objects, groups, events or symbols' (Hogg and Vaughan, 2005: 150);

- 'a psychological tendency that is expressed by evaluating a particular entity with some degree of favor or disfavor' (Eagly and Chaiken, 1993: 1).

Before suggesting this change of terminology here, I used the term 'attitude' rather than 'belief' with my clients and found that it was easier for me to convey the meaning of 'B' when I used 'attitude' than when I used 'belief' and they, in general, found 'attitude' easier to understand in this context than 'belief'.

Consequently, in this book, I will use the term 'attitude'[5] instead of the term 'belief' to denote an evaluative stance taken by a person towards an adversity at 'A' which has emotional, behavioural and thinking implications. In deciding to use the term 'attitude' rather than the term 'belief', I recognise that when it comes to explaining what the 'B' stands for in the ABC framework, the term 'attitude' is problematic because it begins with the letter 'A'. Rather than use an 'AAC' framework which is not nearly as catchy or as memorable as the 'ABC' framework, I suggest using the phrase 'Basic Attitudes'[6] when formally describing 'B' in the ABC framework. While not ideal, this term includes 'attitudes' and indicates that they are central or basic and that they lie at the base of a person's responses to an adversity.

In using the term 'basic', I have thus preserved the letter 'B' so that the well-known 'ABC' framework can be used. However, throughout the book when not formally describing the 'ABC' framework I will employ the word 'attitude' rather than the phrase 'basic attitude' when referring to the particular kind of cognitive processing that REBT argues mediates between an adversity and the person's responses to that negative event.

## 2.2 The Core Nature of Rigid and Flexible Attitudes and Extreme and Non-extreme Attitudes

Before I describe the components and characteristics of rigid and flexible attitudes and of the extreme and non-extreme

---

[5] As this is a new development, please note that other REBT therapists (including myself in my previous work) employ the word 'beliefs'.
[6] This phrase was suggested by my friend and colleague, Walter Matweychuk.

attitudes that are deemed to be derived from them respectively, I will describe the core nature of each of these attitudes.

### 2.2.1   The Core Nature of Rigid and Flexible Attitudes

According the classical theory of REBT (e.g. Ellis, 1994), (1) at the very base of a person's psychologically disturbed responses to an adversity lies a rigid attitude that the person holds towards that adversity and, (2) at the very base of that person's psychologically healthy response to the same adversity lies a flexible attitude. Let me consider the core nature of both a rigid attitude and a flexible attitude.

#### 2.2.1.1 *The Core Nature of a Rigid Attitude*

When a person holds a rigid attitude, its core nature is revealed by the person (a) being *absolute* in allowing no exception to their dictates and, (b) *demanding* that the relevant life conditions that relate to the adversity (including the behaviour of the person themself or that of others) *must* be the way the person wants them to be.

#### 2.2.1.2 *The Core Nature of a Flexible Attitude*

When a person holds a flexible attitude, its core nature is revealed by the person (a) being *relative* in allowing exceptions to their preferences and (b) *preferring* that the relevant life conditions that relate to the adversity (including the behaviour of the person themself or that of others) be the way the person wants them to be, *without demanding* that they must be.

## 2.2.2 The Core Nature of Extreme and Non-extreme Attitudes

According to classical REBT theory (Ellis, 1994), when a person holds a rigid attitude towards an adversity, they are also likely to hold one or more extreme attitudes towards the adversity that are derived from this rigid attitude. When that person holds a flexible attitude towards the same adversity instead, they are also likely to hold one or more non-extreme attitudes towards the adversity that are derived from this flexible attitude.

Let me consider the core nature of both an extreme attitude and a non-extreme attitude.

### 2.2.2.1 *The Core Nature of an Extreme Attitude*

When a person holds an extreme attitude, its core nature is revealed by the person's stance towards the adversity being at the very end of a negative evaluative continuum or even beyond it!

### 2.2.2.2 *The Core Nature of a Non-extreme Attitude*

When a person holds a non-extreme attitude, its core nature is revealed by the person's stance towards the adversity being located between both ends of a negative evaluative continuum.

In the next chapter, I outline and discuss the components and characteristics of rigid and flexible attitudes.

# 3

# The Components and Characteristics of Rigid vs Flexible Attitudes

## 3.1    Introduction

In this chapter, I will outline the components and characteristics of rigid vs. flexible attitudes in that order. I will consider the components of these attitudes first, because it is only possible to understand their characteristics when you understand fully what these attitudes are and, in particular, how rigid attitudes can be distinguished from flexible attitudes.

Albert Ellis (1994), the founder of REBT, who used the term 'beliefs' but meant 'attitudes', argued that there are four main attitudes that explain the existence of psychologically problematic responses to life's adversities. Of these four attitudes, one is rigid and the other three are extreme. As mentioned earlier, rigid attitudes are deemed to lie at the base of these problematic responses. As such, for Ellis and other REBT therapists, they are the most important in accounting for unhealthy responses to life's adversities. I will consider the components and characteristics of these rigid attitudes here and those of the extreme attitudes in the following chapter.

Ellis (1994) also posited that there are four main attitudes that explain the existence of psychologically healthy responses to the same adversities. Of these four attitudes, one is flexible and the other three are non-extreme. As mentioned earlier, flexible attitudes are deemed to lie at the base of these healthy responses. As such, for Ellis and other REBT therapists who take the classical position they are the most important in accounting for healthy responses to life's adversities. I will consider the components and characteristics of these flexible attitudes here and those of the non-extreme attitudes in the following chapter.

## 3.2    The Components and Characteristics of Rigid Attitudes

Rigid attitudes are fixed ideas that you hold about how things absolutely must or must not be. You can hold rigid attitudes towards:

- self (e.g. 'I must be approved');
- others (e.g. 'You must treat me with respect'); or
- life conditions (e.g. 'Life must be fair').

### 3.2.1   The Two Components of Rigid Attitudes

While I have given examples of rigid attitudes in terms of how they are usually expressed, they are made up of two components.

#### 3.2.1.1 *'Asserted Preference' Component*

The first component puts forward what you want and is what I call the 'asserted preference' component as shown in the following:

- 'I want to be approved...'

- 'I want you to treat me with respect…'
- 'I very much want life to be fair…'

### 3.2.1.2 'Demand' Component

The second component transforms this non-rigid 'asserted preference' component into a rigid demand as shown in italics below:

- 'I want to be approved, *and therefore I have to be*';
- 'I want you to treat me with respect, *and therefore you have to do so*';
- 'I very much want life to be fair, *and therefore it has to be the way I want it to be.*'

### 3.2.2   The Four Characteristics of Rigid Attitudes

In this section, I will consider the four characteristics of rigid attitudes. In doing so I will use the following rigid attitude as an example which I will present in its full form: *'I want to do well and therefore it follows that I must do well.'*

### 3.2.2.1 *Rigid Attitudes Are Unconditional*

The word 'must' in this attitude shows that it is unconditional. Thus, note that no conditions are put forward by the person concerned. His attitude is that he has to do well and that's that. If his attitude stated that he had to do well in order to get into university then his attitude would be conditional and thus not rigid and this conditional attitude would not be self-defeating.

### 3.2.2.2 *Rigid Attitudes Are Inconsistent with Reality*

For attitudes to be consistent with reality, they have to describe reality as it existed in the past, as it exists now or as it may exist in the future. When the person holds the rigid attitude that he wants to do well and therefore he has to do well, the first part of his attitude is consistent with reality. It is true that he wants to do well. However, in the second part of the attitude, he is trying to exclude or eradicate the possibility of not doing well.

The reality is that it is not possible for the person to exclude this possibility. It is always *possible* for the person not to do well. Implicitly, the person knows this, since while his rigid attitude is designed to eradicate the possibility of doing poorly in his mind, if he is anxious he recognises that there is such a possibility. Therefore, he is not convinced by his own attempt to eliminate this possibility. He is not allowing himself in his mind the freedom to want to do well, but to do averagely or poorly, which are all possible outcomes in reality. In conclusion, while the first part of his attitude is consistent with reality, the second part isn't and therefore taken as a whole, his rigid attitude is inconsistent with reality.

### 3.2.2.3 *Rigid Attitudes Are Illogical*

If you consider the example of the rigid attitude that I provided, you will see that it is comprised of two parts: (a) *'I want to do well...* (b) *...and therefore it follows that I must do well.'* You will note that the first part of this attitude is non-rigid, while the second part is rigid. Thus, we can say that the attitude is illogical since it attempts to derive something rigid from something that is non-rigid. In addition, when I conclude that I must do well because I want to do well, this conclusion is a non-sequitur as it does not follow logically from my premise of desire.

### 3.2.2.4 *Rigid Attitudes Are Largely Unconstructive*

Once the person holds the rigid attitude in the example given above he will experience a range of consequences, most of which will be unconstructive. First, this attitude will affect the person's emotions. For example, it will lead him to be (1) anxious when he insists he must do well and thinks he may not imminently do well and to be (2) depressed if it transpires that his performance is not as good as he demands rigidly that it must be. Second, holding this attitude will influence how the person behaves. For example, it may lead him to avoid situations where he may not do well, or if he cannot avoid such situations, he may over-prepare his material and may exhaust himself in the process. Finally, this attitude will affect the person's subsequent thinking which will tend to be grossly distorted in a negative direction.[7] For example, when he holds that he must do well and there is a chance that he won't then he will tend to think that he will do very poorly and that the consequences of not doing well will be exceedingly bad. I will discuss the consequences of holding rigid attitudes more fully in Chapter 5.

## 3.3    The Components and Characteristics of Flexible Attitudes

Flexible attitudes are relative ideas that a person holds about how he would like things to be without demanding that they have to be that way. Flexible attitudes can relate to:

---

[7] These cognitive consequences are often viewed as automatic thoughts in Beck's model of cognitive therapy (Wills, 2009).

- self (e.g. 'I want to be approved, but I don't have to be');
- others (e.g. 'I want you to treat me with respect, but regrettably you don't have to do so'); or
- life conditions ('I very much want life to be fair, but unfortunately it doesn't have to be the way I want it to be').

### 3.3.1    The Two Components of Flexible Attitudes

If you look carefully at these attitudes you will see that they are made up of two components.

#### 3.3.1.1 *'Asserted Preference' Component*

The first component is the same as the first component of a rigid attitude and puts forward what the person wants. As I said earlier this is what I call the 'asserted preference' component as shown in the following:

- 'I want to be approved…'
- 'I want you to treat me with respect…'
- 'I very much want life to be fair…'

#### 3.3.1.2 *'Negated Demand' Component*

The second component acknowledges that the person doesn't have to get what he wants and is what I call the 'negated demand' component. These are shown in italics below:

- 'I want to be approved, *but I don't have to be*';
- 'I want you to treat me with respect, *but regrettably you don't have to do so*';

- 'I very much want life to be fair, *but unfortunately it doesn't have to be the way I want it to be.'*

### 3.3.2   The Four Characteristics of Flexible Attitudes

In this section, I will consider the three characteristics of flexible attitudes. In doing so I will use the following flexible attitude as an example which I will present in its full form: *'I want to do well, but I do not have to do well.'*

#### 3.3.2.1 *Flexible Attitudes Are Flexible*

The word 'flexible' means being able to accommodate and adapt to changing circumstances without breaking. Flexible attitudes therefore allow for exceptions to what the person desires and protects the person from developing rigid ideas by stressing that the person does not have to have their preference met.

#### 3.3.2.2 *Flexible Attitudes Are Consistent with Reality*

As I mentioned above, for an attitude to be consistent with reality it has to describe reality as it existed in the past, as it exists now or what is possible is the future. When the person holds that he wants to do well, but that he does not have to do so, the first part of his attitude is consistent with reality since he can prove that he has the desire to do will. In the second part of the attitude he is acknowledging that he may have not done well in the past, that he may not be doing well now and that he may not do well in the future. As such he does not try to exclude or eradicate the possibility of not doing well because he knows that the reality is that it is not possible for him to exclude such a possibility. Thus the second part of his attitude is consistent with reality. Thus, as both parts of the flexible attitude is consistent with reality, it follows that the flexible attitude taken as a whole is consistent with reality.

### 3.3.2.3 *Flexible Attitudes Are Logical*

If you consider the example of flexible attitude that I provided, you will see that it is comprised of two parts: (1) *'I want to do well...* and (2)*... but I do not have to do well'*. You will note that both parts of this belief are non-rigid. Thus, we can say that the belief is logical since it attempts to derive something non-rigid from something that is also non-rigid. Also, when I hold that I want to do well and then conclude that I do not have to do well, then I am being logical as my conclusion follows logically from my premise of desire.

### 3.3.2.4 *Flexible Attitudes Are Largely Constructive*

Once the person holds the flexible attitude in the example given above he will experience a range of consequences most of which will be constructive. First, this attitude will affect the person's emotions. For example, it will lead him to be (1) concerned, but not anxious when he wants, but does not insist, that he must do well and thinks that he may not do well imminently and to be (2) sad, but not depressed if it transpires that his performance is not as good as he would like it to be, but without demanding that it has to be that way. Second, holding this attitude will influence how the person behaves. For example, it will lead him to confront situations where he may not do well without over-preparing his material.

Finally, this attitude will affect how the person's subsequent thinking which will tend to be balanced. For example, when the person holds that he would like to do well, but that he doesn't have to do so and acknowledges that there is a chance that he won't then do well, he will tend to think that while there is a chance that he might not do well, there is also a chance that he will do well. When contemplating that he might not do well, he acknowledges that he may do very poorly but also holds that his performance may be average or slightly poor. Finally, when thinking about the consequences of not doing well, he notes that these may well be exceedingly bad, but also notes that they be minor or even that the consequences may not be bad at all. I will discuss the consequences of holding flexible attitudes more fully in Chapter 5.

In the next chapter, I outline and discuss the components and characteristics of extreme and non-extreme attitudes.

# 4

# The Components and Characteristics of Extreme Attitudes vs Non-extreme Attitudes

## 4.1    Introduction

You will remember that classical REBT theory states that when a person holds a rigid attitude towards an adversity, then that person is also likely to hold one or more extreme attitudes towards the adversity that are derived from this rigid attitude. These are known as: awfulising attitudes, discomfort intolerance attitudes and depreciation attitudes.

When that person holds a flexible attitude towards the same adversity instead, they are also likely to hold one or more non-extreme attitudes towards the adversity that are derived from this flexible attitude. These are known as: non-awfulising attitudes, discomfort tolerance attitudes and acceptance attitudes.

I will first detail the components of each of the three extreme attitudes and their non-extreme alternatives and show what components they have in common and in what ways their components differ. Then I will outline the characteristics of each of these three pairs of attitudes.

## 4.2    The Components and Characteristics of Awfulising Attitudes vs Non-awfulising Attitudes

Awfulising attitudes and non-awfulising attitudes are deemed in REBT theory to stem from rigid attitudes and flexible attitudes respectively.

### 4.2.1    The Components and Characteristics of Awfulising Attitudes

Awfulising attitudes are extreme evaluative ideas that a person holds about how bad it is when their rigid demands are not met. They are thus derivatives from the person's rigid attitudes and as with rigid attitudes, awfulising attitudes relate to self, others and the world. In the following examples the rigid attitudes are listed in brackets:

- '(I must be approved)...It is terrible if I am not approved.'
- '(You must treat me fairly)...It is awful when you treat me with disrespect.'
- '(Life must be comfortable)...It is the end of the world when life is unfair.'

#### 4.2.1.1 *The Two Components of Awfulising Attitudes*

Awfulising attitudes are made up of two components.

##### 4.2.1.1.1    *'Asserted Badness' Component*

The first component puts forward the idea that the person thinks that it is bad when his rigid demands are not met and is what I call the 'asserted badness' component as shown in italics in the following:

- '*It is bad* if I am not approved…..'
- '*It is bad* if you treat me disrespectfully…..'
- '*It is bad* if life is unfair…..'

As can be seen these evaluations of badness are negative in their evaluative nature, but not extreme in this negative evaluation.

### 4.2.1.1.2   *'Awfulising' Component*

The second component transforms this non-extreme 'asserted badness' component into an extreme awfulising attitude. These are shown in italics below:

- 'It is bad if I am not approved *and therefore it is terrible if this happens.*'
- 'It is bad if you treat me disrespectfully *and therefore it is terrible if this happens.*'
- 'It is bad if life is unfair *and therefore it is terrible if this happens.*'

### 4.2.1.2 *The Four Characteristics of Awfulising Attitudes*

In this section, I will consider the four characteristics of awfulising attitudes. In doing so I will use the following awfulising attitude as an example which I will present in its full form: *'It is bad if I do not do well and therefore it follows that it is awful if I do not do well.'*

### 4.2.1.2.1   *Awfulising Attitudes Are Extreme*

Awfulising attitudes stem from rigid attitudes that things must not be as bad as they are and are extreme in the sense that the person holds *at the time* one or more of the following:

1. nothing could be worse;

2. the event in question is worse than 100% bad; and

3. no good could possibly come from this bad event which is wholly bad;

4. the event cannot be transcended.

As can be seen from these statements, awfulising attitudes are, therefore, extreme.

### 4.2.1.2.2   *Awfulising Attitudes Are Inconsistent with Reality*

It is clear from the above meanings of the term 'awful' that when applied to our example an awfulising attitude is false. Thus:

1. Things can be worse for the person than not doing well.

2. It follows from the above that not doing well is not 100% bad.

3. Since the person can learn something productive from not doing well, it follows that the statement 'no good can come from not doing well' is false.

4. The event can be transcended. No matter how bad it is, it is possible for the person to process it and move on with life.

### 4.2.1.2.3  *Awfulising Attitudes Are Illogical*

If you consider the example of an awfulising attitude that I provided, you will see that it is comprised of two parts:

1. 'It is bad if I do not do well...

2. ...and therefore it follows that it is terrible if this happens.'

You will note that the first part of this belief is non-extreme, while the second part is extreme. Thus, we can say that the belief is illogical since it attempts to derive something extreme from something that is non-extreme. In addition, my conclusion that it is terrible if I don't do well is a non-sequitur as it does not follow logically from my premise of badness.

### 4.2.1.2.4  *Awfulising Attitudes Are Largely Unconstructive*

The same points that I outlined with respect to the largely unconstructive effects of rigid attitudes also apply to the largely unconstructive effects of awfulising attitudes (discuss more fully in Chapter 5). Once the person holds the awfulising attitude in the example given above they will experience a range of unconstructive emotive, behavioural and thinking consequences. Thus:

- Emotive – anxiety and depression;
- Behavioural – avoidance and over-preparation;
- Thinking – highly distorted negative predictions.

The healthy alternatives to awfulising attitudes are non-awfulising attitudes.

### 4.2.2 The Components and Characteristics of Non-awfulising Attitudes

Non-awfulising attitudes are non-extreme evaluative ideas that you hold about how bad it is when your flexible preferences are not met. They are thus derivatives from the person's flexible attitudes and as with flexible attitudes, these non-awfulising attitudes relate to self, others and the world. In the following examples the flexible attitudes are in brackets.

- '(I want to be approved, but I don't have to be.) It's bad if I am not approved, but not terrible';
- '(I want you to treat me with respect, but regrettably you don't have to do so.) When you don't treat me with respect, it is bad, but not awful'; and
- '(I very much want life to be fair, but unfortunately it doesn't have to be that way.) If life is unfair, that's very bad, but not the end of the world.'

#### 4.2.2.1 *The Two Components of Non-awfulising Attitudes*

If you look carefully at the non-awfulising attitudes (i.e. the ones that are not in brackets) you will see that they are made up of two components.

##### 4.2.2.1.1 *'Asserted Badness' Component*

The first component puts forward the evaluative idea that it is bad or very bad if you don't get what you want and is what I call the 'asserted badness' component as shown in italics in the following:

- '*It's bad* if I am not approved…';
- 'When you don't treat me with respect, *it's really bad*…'
- If life is unfair, *that's very bad*…'

If you recall, this 'asserted badness' component is also present in an awfulising attitude.

### 4.2.2.1.2   *'Negated Awfulising' Component*

The second component acknowledges that while it is bad if you don't get what you want, it is not terrible, awful or the end of the world. This is what I call the 'negated awfulising' component. These are shown in italics below:

- 'It's bad if I am not approved, *but not terrible* ';
- 'When you don't treat me with respect it's really bad, *but not awful*' and
- 'If life is unfair, that's very bad, *but not the end of the world*'.

### 4.2.2.2   **The Four Characteristics of Non-awfulising Attitudes**

In this section, I will consider the four characteristics of non-awfulising attitudes. In doing so I will use the following non-awfulising attitude as an example which I will present in its full form: **'It is bad if I do not well, but it isn't awful.'**

### 4.2.2.2.1   *Non-awfulising Attitudes Are Non-extreme*

Non-awfulising attitudes are non-extreme in the sense that you believe *at the time* one or more of the following:

- Things could always be worse.
- The event in question is less than 100% bad.
- Good could come from this bad event.
- The event can be transcended.

#### 4.2.2.2.2   *Non-awfulising Attitudes Are Consistent with Reality*

Thus, in our example, the person can prove that there are worse things than not doing well and thus it is less than 100% bad. Also, it is consistent with reality that good can come from not doing well.

#### 4.2.2.2.3   *Non-awfulising Attitudes Are Logical*

If you consider the example of a non-awfulising attitude that I provided earlier, you will see that it is comprised of two parts:

- 'It is bad if I don't do well…
- …but it isn't awful.'

You will note that both parts of this attitude are non-extreme. Thus, we can say that the attitude is logical since it attempts to derive something non-extreme from something that is also non-extreme. In addition, my conclusion that it isn't awful if I don't do well follows logically from my premise of badness and is not a non-sequitur.

#### 4.2.2.2.4   *Non-awfulising Attitudes Are Largely Constructive*

The same points that I outlined with respect to the largely constructive effects of flexible attitudes also apply to the largely constructive effects of non-awfulising attitudes (discussed more fully in Chapter 5). Once the person holds the non-awfulising attitude in the example given above they will experience a range of emotive, behavioural and thinking consequences most of which will be constructive. Thus:

- Emotive – concerned, but not anxious.
- Behavioural – confront situations and not over-preparing material.
- Thinking – balanced thinking concerning future predictions.

## 4.3 The Components and Characteristics of Discomfort Intolerance Attitudes vs Discomfort Tolerance Attitudes

Discomfort intolerance attitudes and discomfort tolerance attitudes are deemed in REBT theory to stem from rigid attitudes and flexible attitudes respectively.

### 4.3.1 The Components and Characteristics of Discomfort Intolerance Attitudes

Discomfort intolerance attitudes are extreme ideas that you hold about the tolerability of events when your rigid demands are not met. They are thus derivatives from the person's rigid attitudes and as with rigid attitudes, they relate to self, others and the world. In the following examples the demands are listed in brackets.

- '(I must be approved). I can't bear it if I am not approved';
- '(You must treat me with respect). It is intolerable when you don't treat me with respect'; and
- '(Life must be fair). I can't stand it when it is unfair.'

### 4.3.1.1  *The Two Components of Discomfort Intolerance Attitudes*

Discomfort intolerance attitudes are made up of two components.

#### 4.3.1.1.1  *'Asserted Struggle' Component*

This first component puts forward the idea that it is difficult tolerating not getting what you want and is what I call the 'asserted struggle' component as shown in italics in the following:

- 'When I am not approved, *it is difficult to bear…'*;
- 'When you don't treat me with respect, *it's really hard to tolerate…'*
- 'If life is uncomfortable, *that's hard to stand…'*

As can be seen these evaluations are non-extreme.

#### 4.3.1.1.2  *'Discomfort Intolerance' Component*

The second component transforms this non-extreme 'asserted struggle' component into an extreme discomfort intolerance attitude. These are shown in italics below:

- 'When I am not approved, it is difficult to bear *and therefore it is unbearable.'*
- 'When you don't treat me with respect, it's really hard to tolerate *and therefore it is intolerable.'*
- 'If life is unfair, that's hard to stand *and therefore I can't stand it.'*

**4.3.1.2** *The Four Characteristics of Discomfort Intolerance Attitudes*

In this section, I will consider the four characteristics of discomfort intolerance attitudes. In doing so I will use the following discomfort intolerance attitude which I will present in its full form: *'It is hard to tolerate not doing well and therefore I can't bear it if I do not do well.'*

4.3.1.2.1   *Discomfort Intolerance Attitudes Are Extreme*

Discomfort intolerance attitudes stem from rigid attitudes that things must not be as bad as they are and are extreme in the sense that the person believes *at the time* one or more of the following:

- I will die or disintegrate if the discomfort or frustration continues to exist.
- I will lose the capacity to experience happiness if the discomfort or frustration continues to exist.

4.3.1.2.2   *Discomfort Intolerance Attitudes Are Inconsistent with Reality*

It is clear from the above that discomfort intolerance attitudes are inconsistent with reality. Thus, in our example:

1. It is easily apparent that the person will neither die nor disintegrate if they do not do well.

2. It is also clear that it is quite possible for the person to experience happiness if they do not do well. Their poor performance does not eradicate their capacity to experience happiness.

### 4.3.1.2.3   *Discomfort Intolerance Attitudes Are Illogical*

If you consider the example of a discomfort intolerance attitude that I provided, you will see that it is comprised of two parts:

1. 'It is hard to tolerate not doing well...

2. ...and therefore I can't bear it if I do not do well.'

You will note that the first part of this attitude is non-extreme, while the second part is extreme. Thus, we can say that a discomfort intolerance attitude is illogical since it attempts to derive something extreme from something that is non-extreme. In addition this attitude's conclusion does not follow from its premise and is therefore an illogical non-sequitur.

### 4.3.1.2.4   *Discomfort Intolerance Attitudes Are Largely Unconstructive*

The same points that I outlined with respect to the largely unconstructive effects of rigid attitudes and awfulising attitudes also apply to the largely unconstructive effects of discomfort intolerance attitudes (discussed more fully in Chapter 5). Once the person holds the discomfort intolerance attitude in the example given above they will experience the same range of emotive, behavioural and thinking consequences that I previously outlined. Thus:

- Emotive – anxiety and depression;
- Behavioural – avoidance and over-preparation;
- Thinking – highly distorted negative predictions.

The healthy alternatives to discomfort intolerance attitudes are discomfort tolerance attitudes.

## 4.3.2 The Components and Characteristics of Discomfort Tolerance Attitudes

Discomfort tolerance attitudes are non-extreme ideas that you hold about the tolerability of events when your flexible preferences are not met. They are thus derivatives from the person's flexible attitudes and as with flexible attitudes, these discomfort tolerance attitudes relate to self, others and the world. In the following examples the flexible attitudes are in brackets.

- '(I want to be approved, but I don't have to be.) When I am not approved it is difficult to bear, but I can bear it and it's worth bearing because I don't want to live my life worried about disapproval. I am therefore willing to experience such disapproval and I am going to do so';

- '(I want you to treat me with respect, but regrettably you don't have to do so.) When you don't treat me with respect it's really hard to tolerate, but I can tolerate it and it's worth it to me to do so because I don't want to be overly affected about what you do. I am therefore prepared to tolerate your disrespectful treatment of me and I am going to do so'; and

- '(I very much want life to be fair, but unfortunately it doesn't have to be the way I want it to be.) If life is uncomfortable, that's hard to stand, but I can stand it and it is in my best interests to do so because I want to get on with life. I am therefore willing to endure such unfairness for as long as it exists and I am going to do so.'

#### 4.3.2.1 *The Five Components of Discomfort Tolerance Attitudes*

If you look carefully at the discomfort tolerance attitudes (i.e. the ones that are not in brackets) you will see that they are made up of five components.

##### 4.3.2.1.1 *'Asserted Struggle' Component*

The first component puts forward the idea that it is difficult tolerating not getting what you want and is what I call the 'asserted struggle' component. This component is shown in italics in the examples below:

- 'When I am not approved, *it is difficult to bear…*'
- 'When you don't treat me with respect, *it's really hard to tolerate…*'
- 'If life is unfair, *that's hard to stand…*'

If you recall, this 'asserted struggle' component is also present in the self-defeating discomfort intolerance attitude.

##### 4.3.2.1.2 *'Negated Unbearability' Component*

The second component acknowledges that while it is a struggle to put up with what you don't want, it is possible to do so and that it is not unbearable. This is what I call the 'negated unbearability' component. This component is shown in italics in the examples below:

- 'When I am not approved it is difficult to bear, *but I can bear it…*'
- 'When you don't treat me fairly it's really hard to tolerate, *but I can tolerate it…*'

- 'If life is uncomfortable, that's hard to stand, *but I can stand it...*'

#### 4.3.2.1.3 'Worth Bearing' Component

The third component addresses the point that it is often worth it to you to tolerate the situation where you don't get what you want. This is what I call the 'worth bearing' component. This component is shown in italics in the examples below. Note that in each case the reason why it is worth tolerating is specified.

- 'When I am not approved it is difficult to bear, but I can bear it *and it's worth bearing* because I don't want to live my life worried about disapproval';
- 'When you don't treat me with respect it's really hard to tolerate, but I can tolerate it *and it's worth it to me to do so* because I don't want to be overly affected about what you do'; and
- If life is unfair, that's hard to stand, but I can stand it and *it is in my best interests to do so* because I want to get on with life.'

#### 4.3.2.1.4 'Willingness to Endure It' Component

The fourth component indicates the person's willingness to endure discomfort. This is a really important component that has largely been neglected by REBT therapists, but has been emphasised by theorists and practitioners of Acceptance and Commitment Therapy (Hayes, Strosahl and Wilson, 1999). Thus, it is possible for a person to acknowledge (a) that it is a struggle to endure discomfort, (b) that it is possible to do so and (c) that it is in their interests to do just that, but for the person to decide not to endure it partly because they have not made it clear with themselves that they are willing to endure it. This component is shown in italics in the examples below:

- 'When I am not approved it is difficult to bear, but I can bear it and it's worth bearing because it is very handicapping to live my life worried about disapproval. *I am therefore willing to experience such disapproval*';
- 'When you don't treat me with respect it's really hard to tolerate, but I can tolerate it and it's worth it to me to do so because I don't want to be overly affected about what you do. *I am therefore prepared to tolerate your disrespectful treatment of me*'; and
- 'If life is unfair, that's hard to stand, but I can stand it and it is in my best interests to do so because I want to get on with life. *I am therefore willing to endure such discomfort.*'

### 4.3.2.1.5 'Behavioural Commitment to Endure It' Component

While introducing the willingness to endure component is important, there is one more component to be added for the person to translate such willingness into action. This involves the person making a commitment to act on one's willingness. This, in my view is 'the icing on the cake' and roots the other four components in a behavioural decision missing in these components as shown in italics in the following statements:

- 'When I am not approved it is difficult to bear, but I can bear it and it's worth bearing because I don't want to live

my life worried about disapproval. I am therefore
willing to experience such disapproval *and I am going to
do so'*;

- 'When you don't treat me fairly it's really hard to
tolerate, but I can tolerate it and it's worth it to me to do
so because I don't want to be overly affected about what
you do. I am therefore prepared to tolerate your unfair
treatment of me *and I am going to do so'*; and

- 'If life is unfairness, that's hard to stand, but I can stand
it and it is in my best interests to do so because I want to
get on with life. I am therefore willing to endure such
unfairness. *and I am going to do so until I can do something
about it or it ceases to exist.'*

## 4.3.2.2 The Four Characteristics of Discomfort Tolerance
   Attitudes

In this section, I will consider the four characteristics of
discomfort tolerance attitudes. In doing so I will use the
following discomfort tolerance attitude as an example which
I will present in its full form: *'It is difficult for me to tolerate
it when I do not do well, but I can tolerate it and it is worth
it to me to do so. I am thus willing to endure it and I am
going to do so.'*

### 4.3.2.2.1   *Discomfort Tolerance Attitudes Are Non-extreme*

Discomfort tolerance attitudes are non-extreme in the sense
that you believe *at the time* one or more of the following:

1. I will struggle if the discomfort or frustration
   continues to exist, but I will neither die nor
   disintegrate;

2. I will not lose the capacity to experience some happiness if the discomfort or frustration continues to exist, although this capacity will be temporarily diminished; and

3. The frustration or discomfort is worth tolerating, all things considered;

4. I have a choice whether to tolerate it or not.

#### 4.3.2.2.2 *Discomfort Tolerance Attitudes Are Consistent with Reality*

Discomfort tolerance attitudes are true in that the person can prove all components of the attitude as listed above.

#### 4.3.2.2.3 *Discomfort Tolerance Attitudes Are Logical*

If you consider the example of a discomfort tolerance attitude that I provided earlier, you will see that it is comprised of five parts:

1. 'It is difficult for me to tolerate it when I do not well…'
2. ' … but I can tolerate it…
3  … and it is worth it to me to do so.'
4. 'I am willing to endure it.'
5. 'I am going to endure it.'

You will note that all five parts of this attitude are non-extreme. Thus, we can say that the belief is logical since it attempts to derive things that are non-extreme from something that is also non-extreme.

4.3.2.2.4   *Discomfort   Tolerance   Attitudes   Are   Largely   Constructive*

The same points that I outlined with respect to the largely constructive effects of flexible attitudes and non-awfulising attitudes also apply to the largely constructive effects of discomfort tolerance attitudes (discussed more fully in Chapter 5). Once the person holds the discomfort tolerance attitude in the example given above they will experience a range of emotive, behavioural and thinking consequences most of which will be constructive. Thus:

* Emotive – concerned, but not anxious;
* Behavioural – confront situations and not over-preparing material;
* Thinking – balanced thinking concerning future predictions.

## 4.4   The Components and Characteristics of Depreciation Attitudes vs Acceptance Attitudes

Depreciation beliefs and acceptance beliefs are deemed in REBT theory to stem from rigid attitudes and flexible attitudes respectively.

### 4.4.1   The Components and Characteristics of Depreciation Attitudes

Depreciation attitudes are extreme overgeneralised ideas that you hold about self, other(s) and/or the world when you don't get what you rigidly demand that you must get. As such, and as stated above, depreciation attitudes are derivatives from your rigid attitudes. In the following examples the rigid attitudes are listed in brackets.

- '(I must be approved.) I am worthless if am not approved.'
- '(You must treat me with respect.) You are a bad person if you don't treat me fairly.'
- '(Life must be fair.) Life is bad if it is not fair.'

### 4.4.1.1 *The Two Components of Depreciation Attitudes*

Depreciation attitudes are often made up of two components.

#### 4.4.1.1.1   *'Aspect Evaluation' Component*

The first component evaluates an aspect of a person (self or other), an aspect of life or an aspect of what happens to the person and is what I call the 'aspect evaluation' component as is shown in italics in the following:

- 'When I am not approved, *it is bad*...'
- 'When you don't treat me with respect, *it's really bad* ...'
- 'If life is unfair, *that is unfortunate*...'

As can be seen these evaluations are non-extreme.

#### 4.4.1.1.2   *'Whole Evaluation' Component*

The second component transforms this non-extreme 'aspect evaluation' component into an extreme overgeneralised depreciation attitude. These are shown in italics below:

- 'When I am not approved, it is bad *and therefore I am worthless.'*
- 'When you don't treat me with respect fairly, it's really bad *and therefore you are a bad person.'*
- 'If life is unfair, that is unfortunate *and therefore life is no good.'*

### 4.4.1.2 *The Four Characteristics of Depreciation Attitudes*

In this section, I will consider the four characteristics of depreciation attitudes. In doing so I will use the following depreciation attitude as an example which I will present in its full form: *'It is bad when I do not do well and therefore I am worthless if this happens.'*

#### 4.4.1.2.1 *Depreciation Attitudes Are Extreme*

Depreciation attitudes stem from rigid attitudes that you, others and things must be as you want them to be and are extreme in the sense that you hold *at the time* one or more of the following:

1. A person (self or other) can legitimately be given a single global rating that defines their essence and the worth of a person is dependent upon conditions that change (e.g. my worth goes up when I do well and goes down when I don't do well).

2. The world can legitimately be given a single rating that defines its essential nature and that the value of the world varies according to what happens within it (e.g. the value of the world goes up when something fair occurs and goes down when something unfair happens).

3. A person can be rated on the basis of one of his or her aspects and the world can be rated on the basis of one of its aspects.

### 4.4.1.2.2  *Depreciation Attitudes Are Inconsistent with Reality*

It is clear from the above that the depreciation attitude in our example is inconsistent with reality. If the person does not do well it is true to say that this is bad, but entirely false to say that they are worthless. For it to be true that the person is worthless, everything would have to be worthless about them: now, in the past and in the future. Thus, it is inconsistent with reality to say that the person can be legitimately rated on the basis of one or some arbitrarily selected set of aspects or experiences.

### 4.4.1.2.3  *Depreciation Attitudes Are Illogical*

If you consider the example of a depreciation attitude that I provided, you will see that it is comprised of two parts:

1. 'It is bad when I do not do well....

2. ...and therefore I am worthless if this happens.'

You will note that the first part of this attitude is non-extreme, while the second part is extreme. Thus, we can say that the attitude is illogical since it attempts to derive something extreme from something that is non-extreme. Also, I am making the illogical part-whole error here in that I am defining the whole of me on the basis of an aspect of me.

### 4.4.1.2.4  *Depreciation Attitudes Are Largely Unconstructive*

The same points that I outlined with respect to the largely unconstructive effects of rigid attitudes, awfulising attitudes and discomfort intolerance attitudes also apply to the largely unconstructive effects of depreciation attitudes (discussed more fully in Chapter 5). Once the person holds the depreciation attitude in the example given above they will experience a range of emotive, behavioural and thinking consequences most of which will again be unconstructive. Thus:

- Emotive – anxiety and depression;
- Behavioural – avoidance and over-preparation;
- Thinking – highly distorted negative predictions.

The healthy alternative to a depreciation attitude is an acceptance attitude.

### 4.4.2 The Components and Characteristics of Acceptance Attitudes

Acceptance attitudes are non-extreme ideas that you hold about self, other(s) and/or the world when you don't get what you want, but do not demand that you have to get want you want. As such, acceptance attitudes are derivatives from your flexible attitudes. In the following examples, the flexible attitudes are in brackets:

- '(I want to be approved, but I don't have to be.) When I am not approved that is bad, but I am not worthless. I am a fallible human being who is not being approved on this occasion.'
- '(I want you to treat me with respect, but regrettably you don't have to do so.) When you don't treat me with respect that is very unfortunate, but you are not a bad person. Rather, you are a fallible human being who is treating me disrespectfully.'

- '(I very much want life to be fair, but unfortunately it doesn't have to be the way I want it to be.) If life is unfair it is only unfair in this respect and that is unfortunate, but doesn't prove that life is rotten. Life is a complex mixture of the fair, the unfair and the neutral.'

### 4.4.2.1 *The Three Components of Acceptance Attitudes*

If you look carefully at the acceptance attitudes (i.e. the ones that are not in brackets), you will see that they are made up of three components.

#### 4.4.2.1.1   *'Aspect Evaluation' Component*

The first component acknowledges that it is possible and realistic to evaluate a part of a person or what has happened to that person as shown in italics below:

- When I am not approved *that is bad...*
- When you don't treat me with respect *that is very regrettable...*
- If life is unfair it is only unfair in this respect *and that is unfortunate...*

If you recall, this 'aspect evaluation' component is also present in an overgeneralised depreciation attitude.

#### 4.4.2.1.2   *'Negation of Depreciation' Component*

The second component puts forward the idea that it is not possible to evaluate globally a person or life conditions when you don't get what you want, while not demanding that you have to get it. I call this the 'negation of depreciation' component. These are shown in italics below:

- When I am not approved that is bad, *but I am not worthless...*'

- 'When you don't treat me with respect that is very regrettable, *but you are not a bad person...*'

- 'If life is unfair it is only unfair in this respect and that is unfortunate, *but doesn't prove that life is rotten...*'

### 4.4.2.1.3  *'Assertion of Acceptance' Component*

The third component asserts the idea that when you don't get what you want, but do not demand that you have to get it, this does not affect the fallibility of people and the complexity of life. This is what I call the 'assertion of acceptance' component. These are shown in italics below:

- 'When I am not approved that is bad, but I am not worthless. *I am a fallible human being who is not being approved on this occasion.*'

- 'When you don't treat me with respect that is very regrettable, but you are not a bad person. *Rather you are a fallible human being who is treating me disrespectfully.*'

- 'If life is unfair it is only unfair in this respect and that is unfortunate, but doesn't prove that life is rotten. *Life is complex where many fair, unfair and neutral things take place.*'

### 4.4.2.2 *The Four Characteristics of Acceptance Attitudes*

In this section, I will consider the four characteristics of acceptance attitudes. In doing so I will use the following acceptance attitude as an example which I will present in its full form: *'It is bad when I do not do well, but it does not prove that I am worthless. I am a fallible human being who has not done well on this occasion.'*

### 4.4.2.2.1   *Acceptance Attitudes Are Non-extreme*

Acceptance attitudes are non-extreme in the sense that you believe *at the time* one or more of the following:

1. A person cannot legitimately be given a single global rating that defines their essence and their worth, as far as they have it, is not dependent upon conditions that change (e.g. my worth stays the same whether or not I do well).

2. Life cannot legitimately be given a single rating that defines its essential nature and that the value of life does not vary according to what happens within it (e.g. the value of life stays the same whether fairness exists at any given time or not).

3. It makes sense to rate discrete aspects of a person and of the world, but it does not make sense to rate a person or the world on the basis of these discrete aspects.

### 4.4.2.2.2   *Acceptance Attitudes Are Consistent with Reality*

The acceptance attitude in our example is true in that the person can prove all three components of the attitude as listed above. Thus, the person can prove:

   (a) It is bad when he does not do well.

   (b) He is not worthless when he does not do well.

(c) He is a fallible human being when he does not do well.

### 4.4.2.2.3 *Acceptance Attitudes Are Logical*

If you consider the example of an acceptance attitude that I provided earlier, you will see that it is comprised of three parts:

(a) 'It is bad when I do not do well.'

(b) 'I am not worthless when I do not do well.'

(c) 'I am a fallible human being when I do not do well.'

You will note that all three parts of this attitude are non-extreme. Thus, we can say that the attitude is logical since it attempts to derive things that are non-extreme from something that is also non-extreme. Also, this attitude is logical because each part follows logically from the preceding part. No part is logically contradicted by any other part.

### 4.4.2.2.4 *Acceptance Beliefs Are Largely Constructive*

The same points that I outlined with respect to the largely constructive effects of flexible attitudes, non-awfulising attitudes and discomfort tolerance attitudes apply to the largely constructive effects of acceptance attitudes (discussed fully in Chapter 5). Once the person holds the acceptance attitude in the example given above, they will experience a range of emotive, behavioural and thinking consequences most of which will be constructive. Thus:

- Emotive – concerned, but not anxious;
- Behavioural – confront situations and not over-preparing material;
- Thinking – balanced thinking concerning future predictions.

Having discussed the characteristics and component structure of rigid and extreme attitudes and flexible and non-extreme attitudes, I will now turn my attention to the consequences of both sets of attitudes.

# 5

# The Consequences of Holding Rigid and Extreme Attitudes and Flexible and Non-Extreme Attitudes

## 5.1   Introduction

When discussing the characteristics of rigid and extreme attitudes, on the one hand and of flexible and non-extreme attitudes, on the other, I have made the point that the consequences of holding the former are largely unconstructive and the consequences of holding the latter are largely constructive. In this concluding chapter, I will build on this point and discuss the psychological consequences of holding both sets of attitudes with respect to a variety of adversities that people are encounter in life with respect to their personal domain (Beck, 1976). You will see quite clearly that when people hold rigid and extreme attitudes towards life's adversities then they will experience a range of disturbed responses towards these eventualities, but when they hold flexible and non-extreme attitudes towards the same adversities then they will respond healthily to them.

## 5.2   The Personal Domain

Before I consider the consequences of holding rigid and extreme attitudes about adversities, on the one hand and flexible and non-extreme attitudes about these same adversities, on the other, I want to introduce a concept which is important to understand if you are to comprehend fully the nature of an adversity. This concept is known as the 'personal domain'. Beck (1976: 54) said that 'the objects – tangible and intangible – in which a person has an involvement constitute his personal domain'. The more involvement the person has with one such object, the more central a place it occupies in their personal domain. Beck (1976: 56) went on to say that 'the nature of a person's emotional response – or emotional disturbance – depends on whether he perceives events as adding to, subtracting from, endangering or impinging upon his domain'. Therefore, the relationship between what happens to the person and their personal domain is key to understanding whether that event will be seen as an adversity or not.

### 5.2.1   Descriptions and Inferences

When an event occurs it is important to distinguish between a description of the event and an inference that the person makes of the event with respect to their personal domain.

#### 5.2.1.1 *Descriptions*

When something happens to a person, it is possible for that person to describe what has happened to them. Now such a description may be accurate or inaccurate, but its defining characteristic is that it does not add any inferential meaning. Thus, let's suppose my boss asks to see me and says that in his view the report that I wrote for him was 'OK, not great, but OK'. Later, I am asked by a colleague to relate what happened. If I say, 'My boss said that the report I wrote for him was OK, not great, but OK', then I am giving a description of what he said that was accurate.

### 5.2.1.2 *Inferences*

In the example, I gave above, if I said in reply to colleague's question that 'my boss criticised the report that I wrote for him', I would be making a statement that goes beyond the data at hand and ascribes an attitude to the boss's view of my work. Such statements are known as inferences.

There are four important features of inferences that need to be kept in mind in the ensuing discussion of the consequences of rigid and extreme attitudes, on the one hand, and of flexible and non-extreme attitudes, on the other.

- Inferences need to be regarded as hypotheses that need testing against the available data rather than as facts.
- Inferences may be accurate or inaccurate. In general, when considering what constitutes an adversity for a person and understanding the factors involved in their disturbed response, we assume temporarily that the person's inference is correct.
- Inferences need to be considered with respect to their relationship with the personal domain of the person concerned.
- Specific inferences often reflect a more general inferential theme. As will be shown below, different inferential themes occur in different emotions.

## 5.3 Psychologically Unhealthy Responses to Adversities and Their Healthy Alternatives

In this section, I will consider the main problematic responses to adversities that people experience and for which they seek help. These are: anxiety, depression, guilt, shame hurt, problematic anger, problematic jealousy and problematic envy. These are all deemed to be based on rigid and extreme attitudes that people hold about a range of adversities that I will also list. After each unhealthy negative emotion (as they are known in REBT) I will consider the healthy negative emotion alternative. All these healthy negative emotions are deemed to be based on flexible and non-extreme attitudes that people hold about the same adversities that are featured in the unhealthy negative emotions. They are concern, sadness, remorse, disappointment, sorrow, non-problematic anger, non-problematic jealousy and non-problematic envy. For each unhealthy and healthy negative emotion, I will list the behaviours and thinking that are associated with them.

Before I proceed, let me say a word about language, while I listed a number of terms denoting what REBT theorists and practitioners refer to as 'healthy negative emotions', it is important to emphasise that this language is not universally accepted. Although this is a book on theory not practice, it is important with fellow theorists and clients that you establish a common language before continuing with theoretical or clinical discussions.

REBT theory distinguishes between ego disturbance and non-ego disturbance (Dryden, 1999). Ego disturbance is primarily based on a rigid attitude and an overgeneralised self-depreciation extreme attitude and non-ego disturbance is primarily based on a rigid attitude and at least one extreme attitude that does not involve self-appraisals (e.g. awfulising, discomfort intolerance, other-depreciation and life-depreciation attitudes). I will make clear what the major flexible and non-extreme attitudes are that underpin each of the eight painful and healthy emotions listed above.

By contrast, REBT theory also distinguishes between ego health and non-ego health (Dryden, Gordon and Neenan, 1997). Ego health is primarily based on a flexible attitude and a self-acceptance non-extreme attitude and non-ego disturbance is primarily based on a flexible attitude and at least one non-extreme attitude that does not involve self-appraisals (e.g. non-awfulising, discomfort tolerance, other-acceptance and life-acceptance attitudes). I will make clear what the major flexible and non-extreme attitudes are that underpin each of the eight painful and healthy emotions listed above.

### 5.3.1 Anxiety and Concern

In this section, I will consider the ABCs of anxiety and concern in that order.

#### 5.3.1.1 *Anxiety*

##### 5.3.1.1.1 *The Major Inference Theme in Anxiety ('A')*

When a person is anxious, they are facing or think they are facing a *threat* to some aspect of their personal domain which if you recall is the psychological space where 'the objects – tangible and intangible – in which a person has an involvement' (Beck, 1976: 54) are located. There are different forms of anxiety which I will list in Table 5.1 together with the typical threats that feature in them.

Ellis (1979, 1980) distinguished between two types of anxiety: ego anxiety and discomfort anxiety. In the first, people infer the presence of threats to their self-esteem (e.g. failure, disapproval, rejection, loss of status) while in the latter, people infer the presence of threats to their level of comfort (e.g. loss of self-control, uncertainty that one is not safe from threat, experiencing discomfort, loss of order and experiencing certain internal processes – e.g. unwanted thoughts, feelings, images and urges).

**Table 5.1**   Different types of anxiety (at 'C') and their major inference themes (at 'A')

| Type of anxiety ('C') | Typical threats ('A') |
|---|---|
| Social anxiety | • Acting poorly in a social setting (e.g. revealing that you are anxious; saying something stupid; not knowing what to say)<br>• Being judged negatively by people |
| Health anxiety | • Being uncertain that a symptom that you have is not malignant |
| Generalised anxiety | • A general sense that you do not know that you are safe<br>• A general sense that something may happen which will result in you losing self-control in some way<br>• Thinking that you may become anxious |
| Public speaking anxiety | • Performing poorly while the focus of the audience is on you (e.g. going blank; revealing that you are anxious)<br>• Being judged negatively by people |
| Test anxiety | • Doing poorly on the test<br>• Going blank |
| Panic | • Not knowing that you will regain self-control immediately in a situation where you have begun to lose it |

### 5.3.1.1.2 *Rigid and Extreme Attitudes in Anxiety ('B')*

In ego anxiety, a person holds a rigid attitude and an extreme self-depreciation attitude towards threats to ego aspects of their personal domain. In non-ego anxiety, a person holds a rigid attitude and one or more of the following extreme attitudes: awfulising, discomfort intolerance, other-depreciation and life-depreciation.

### 5.3.1.1.3 *Behaviour Associated with Anxiety (Behavioural 'C')*

When a person holds a rigid and an extreme attitude towards a threat to their personal domain, they will experience anxiety and will act or tend to act in a number of ways, the most common of which are as follows:

- They avoid the threat.
- They withdraw physically from the threat.
- They ward off the threat (e.g. by rituals or superstitious behaviour).
- They try and neutralise the threat (e.g. by being nice to rather than stand up to people of whom they are afraid).
- They distract themself from the threat by engaging in other activity.
- They keep checking on the current status of the threat hoping to find that it has disappeared or become benign.
- They seek reassurance from others that the threat is benign.
- They seek support from others so that if the threat happens these others will handle it or be there to rescue them.

- They over-prepare in order to minimise the threat happening or so that they are prepared to meet it (N.B. it is the over-preparation that is the problem here).

- They tranquillise their feelings so that they don't think about the threat or feel anxious.

- They over-compensate for feeling vulnerable by seeking out an even greater threat to prove to themselves that they can cope.

You will see from the above list, the main purpose of most of these behaviours (and action tendencies, which are urges to behave which the person has not yet converted into overt behaviour) is to keep the person safe from the threat. However, such safety-seeking behaviour is largely responsible for the maintenance of anxiety since it prevents the person from (a) facing up to the situation in which they think that the threat exists and dealing with the threat if it does exist; or from (b) seeing that their inference of threat is inaccurate.

### 5.3.1.1.4   *Thinking Associated with Anxiety (Cognitive 'C')*

When a person holds a rigid and extreme attitude towards a threat to their personal domain then they will feel anxious and will tend to think in a number of ways. There are two types of post-rigid and extreme attitude thinking at play here: threat-exaggerating thinking and safety-seeking thinking.

It is important to note that in both types of post-rigid and extreme attitude thinking, such thinking may be in words or in mental images. As an example of the latter, the person pictures everyone laughing at them if they make a mistake in public.

(a) *Threat-exaggerating thinking.* In the first type of post-rigid and extreme attitude thinking that is associated with anxiety – that I have called 'threat-exaggerating thinking' – the person elaborates and magnifies the threat and its consequences in their mind as shown below:

- They overestimate the probability of the threat occurring.
- They underestimate their ability to cope with the threat.
- They selectively attend to threat both externally and internally.
- They ruminate about the threat.
- They create an even more negative threat in their mind.
- They magnify the negative consequences of the threat and minimise its positive consequences.
- They have more task-irrelevant thoughts than in concern.

(b) *Safety-seeking thinking.* The second type of post-rigid and extreme attitude thinking that is associated with anxiety is the cognitive version of behaviour that is designed to keep the person safe in the moment. I call this form of thinking 'safety-seeking thinking'. Here are some common examples:

- They withdraw mentally from the threat.
- They try to persuade themself that the threat is not imminent and that they are 'imagining' it.
- They think in ways designed to reassure themself that the threat is benign or, if not, that its consequences will be insignificant.

- They distract themself from the threat, e.g. by focusing on mental scenes of safety and well-being.
- They over-prepare mentally in order to minimise the threat happening or so that they are prepared to meet it (N.B. once again it is the over-preparation that is the problem here).
- They picture themself dealing with the threat in an unrealistic overly masterful way.
- They overcompensate for their feeling of vulnerability by picturing themself dealing effectively with an even bigger threat.

One important point to note about these two forms of post-rigid and extreme attitude thinking is that they are quite different: in one the person elaborates and magnifies the threat and in the other they are thinking of ways to protect themself against the threat. People can, and often do, switch rapidly between these different forms of thinking. The more a person's safety-seeking thinking fails to keep themself safe, the more they will mentally elaborate and magnify the threat and the more they do the latter, the more they will try to search mentally for safety.

### 5.3.1.2 Concern

The healthy alternative to anxiety is concern.

#### 5.3.1.2.1  *The Major Inference Theme in Concern ('A')*

When a person is concerned, but not anxious, they are facing or think they are facing the same *threat* to some aspect of their personal domain as when they are anxious.

### 5.3.1.2.2   *Flexible and Non-extreme Attitudes in Concern ('B')*

In ego concern, a person holds a flexible attitude and a non-extreme self-acceptance attitude towards threats to ego aspects of their personal domain. In non-ego concern, a person holds a flexible attitude and one or more of the following non-extreme attitudes: non-awfulising, discomfort tolerance, other-acceptance and life-acceptance.

### 5.3.1.2.3   *Behaviour Associated with Concern (Behavioural 'C')*

When a person holds a flexible and a non-extreme attitude towards a threat to their personal domain, they will experience concern and will act or tend to act in a number of ways, the most common of which are as follows:

- They face up to the threat without using any safety-seeking measures.

- They take constructive action to deal with the threat.

- They seek support from others to help them face up to the threat and then take constructive action by themself rather than rely on others to handle it for them.

- They prepare to meet the threat but do not over-prepare.

You will see from the above list, the main purpose of most of these behaviours (and action tendencies) is to help the person face up to and deal with the threat without the use of safety-seeking behaviour and to gauge if their inference of threat is accurate or inaccurate. You will also note that this list is much shorter than the list outlining the behaviours that are associated with anxiety. The reason is that when you seek safety from threat there are far more ways of doing so than when you face up to the threat.

5.3.1.2.4 *Thinking Associated with Concern (Cognitive 'C')*

When a person holds a flexible and a non-extreme attitude towards a threat to their personal domain then they will feel non-anxious, but concerned and will tend think in a number of ways:

- They are realistic about the probability of the threat occurring.

- They view the threat realistically.

- They realistically appraise their ability to cope with the threat.

- They think about what to do concerning dealing with threat constructively rather than ruminate about the threat.

- They have more task-relevant thoughts than in anxiety.

As the above list shows, the dominant features of thinking associated with concern are that it is realistic and coping-focused. Thus, when a person is concerned, but not anxious, they do not elaborate or magnify the threat and nor do they mentally seek safety from it. Please remember that such thinking may be in words or in mental pictures. In the latter, for example, the person pictures themself initially struggling with the threat, but eventually dealing with it productively.

## 5.3.2  Depression and Sadness

In this section, I will consider the ABCs of depression and sadness in that order.

## 5.3.2.1 *Depression*

Here, I am mainly referring to unipolar depression rather than bipolar disorder (David, Szentagotai, Lupu and Cosman, 2008).

### 5.3.2.1.1  *The Major Inference Themes in Depression ('A')*

Before, I consider the major inference themes in depression, let me state that there are three realms of a person's personal domain that are implicated in depression.

(a) *The Autonomous Realm.* Here the person values such things as freedom from influence, freedom from constraint, freedom to determine one's fate, independence, self-control and effective functioning (Beck, Epstein and Harrison, 1983).

(b) *The Sociotropic Realm.* Here the person values such things as their relationships with people, their connection to them, being loved, being approved, being cared for by them, being able to rely on them and also being able to look after them (Beck, Epstein and Harrison, 1983).

(c) *The Deservingness Realm.* Here the person values themself and others being treated fairly by the world (Hauck, 1973).

Having outlined the three major realms of the personal domain where depression is experienced, I will now outline the three main inference themes in depression. When a person is depressed, they infer at 'A' in the ABC framework:

*   a *loss* from the sociotropic and/or autonomous realms of their personal domain;

- a *failure* within the sociotropic and/or autonomous realms of their personal domain;

- that they or others have experienced an *undeserved plight* in the deservingness realm of their personal domain.

### 5.3.2.1.2   *Rigid and Extreme Attitudes in Depression*

The rigid and extreme attitudes that REBT hypothesises are at the base of depression are, as you will see, at the base of each of the eight disturbed emotions that I will discuss here. They can thus be regarded as a transdiagnostic process in that they represent an aspect of cognition that contributes to the maintenance of a variety of psychological disorders (Harvey, Watkins, Mansell and Shafran, 2004).

While a rigid attitude is regarded by REBT as lying at the base of depression, the extreme attitudes that are derived from the rigid attitude often distinguish between whether a person is experiencing ego depression (where the person depreciates themself) and non-ego depression (where the person holds an awfulising attitude or finds the adversity intolerable). A person may, of course, experience both ego depression and non-ego depression in a given situation.

### 5.3.2.1.3   *Behaviour Associated with Depression (Behavioural 'C')*

When a person holds a rigid and an extreme attitude towards a loss, failure or undeserved plight within the relevant realm of their personal domain then they will feel depressed and then act or tend to act in a number of ways, the most common of which are as follows:

- They withdraw from reinforcements.
- They withdraw into themself (particularly in autonomous depression).
- They become overly dependent on and seek to cling to others (particularly in sociotropic depression).
- They bemoan their fate or that of others to anyone who will listen (particularly in pity-based depression).
- They create an environment consistent with their depressed feelings. For example, their home is dark and bleak.
- They attempt to terminate feelings of depression in self-destructive ways (e.g. drug use).

It can be seen from the above list that these behaviours get in the way of the person processing loss, failure or undeserved plight so that they can grieve appropriately, integrate it into their system of attitudes and change what can be changed and then move on with pursuing their life's goals.

### 5.3.2.1.4 *Thinking Associated with Depression (Cognitive 'C')*

When a person holds a rigid and an extreme attitude towards a loss, failure or undeserved plight they will feel depressed and then think in a number of ways. Below is a list of this post–rigid and extreme attitude depressed thinking:

- The person sees only negative aspects of the loss, failure or undeserved plight.
- They think of other losses, failures and undeserved plights that they (and in the case of the latter, others) have experienced.

- They think they are unable to help themself (helplessness).
- They only see pain and blackness in the future (hopelessness).
- They see themself being too dependent for their liking on others (in autonomous depression).
- They see themself as being too disconnected for their liking from others (in sociotropic depression).
- They see the world as too full of undeservedness and unfairness (in plight-based depression).
- They tend to ruminate concerning the source of their depression and its consequences.

As you can see, such thinking exaggerates the negativity of loss, failure and undeserved plight and the consequences of each and may be in words or in mental images. As an example of the latter, the person pictures themself helpless having lost their job

### 5.3.2.2 *Sadness*

The healthy alternative to depression is sadness.

#### 5.3.2.2.1 *The Major Inference Themes in Sadness ('A')*

When a person is sad, but not depressed, they infer at 'A' in the ABC framework:

- a *loss* from the sociotropic and/or autonomous realms of their personal domain;
- a *failure* within the sociotropic and/or autonomous realms of their personal domain;

- that they or others have experienced an *undeserved plight* in the deservingness realm of their personal domain.

### 5.3.2.2.2  *Flexible and Non-extreme Attitudes in Sadness*

In ego sadness, a person holds a flexible attitude and a non-extreme self-acceptance attitude towards loss and failure. In non-ego sadness, a person holds a flexible attitude and one or more of the following non-extreme attitudes towards, loss, failure and undeserved plight: non-awfulising, discomfort tolerance, other-acceptance and life-acceptance.

### 5.3.2.2.3  *Behaviour Associated with Sadness (Behavioural 'C')*

When a person holds a flexible and a non-extreme attitude towards a loss from one's personal domain, a failure or an undeserved plight within the domain, they will experience sadness and will act or tend to act in a number of ways, the most common of which are as follows:

- They seek out reinforcements after a period of mourning (particularly when their inferential theme is loss).
- They create an environment inconsistent with depressed feelings. For example, there home is full of light and colour.
- They express their feelings about the loss, failure or undeserved plight and talk in a non-complaining way about their feelings to significant others.

### 5.3.2.2.4  *Thinking Associated with Sadness (Cognitive 'C')*

When a person holds a flexible and a non-extreme attitude towards a loss, failure or undeserved plight then they will feel sadness, but not depressed and will tend to think in a number of ways:

- They are able to recognise both negative and positive aspects of the loss or failure.
- They think they are not helpless and can benefit from using their own resources and that others can help them.
- They look to the future with hope.

As the above list shows, the dominant features of thinking associated with sadness are that it is realistic and optimistic. Please remember again that such thinking may be in words or in mental pictures. As an example of the latter the person pictures helping themself once they have gotten over the shock of losing their job.

### 5.3.3     Guilt and Remorse

In this section, I will consider the ABCs of guilt and remorse in that order.

#### 5.3.3.1 *Guilt*

##### 5.3.3.1.1    *The Major Inference Themes in Guilt ('A')*

The three major themes in relation to a person's personal domain that are implicated in guilt are as follows; The person has or thinks they have:

- *broken their moral code* (i.e. they have done the wrong thing);
- *failed to live up to their moral code* (i.e. they failed to do the right thing);
- *hurt someone's feelings.*

### 5.3.3.1.2 *Rigid and Extreme Attitudes in Guilt*

In guilt the person holds the rigid attitude that they absolutely should not have broken or failed to live up to their moral code or that they absolutely should not have hurt someone's feelings and their main extreme attitude is self-depreciation in the moral realm e.g. some variant of 'I'm bad'.

### 5.3.3.1.3 *Behaviour Associated with Guilt (Behavioural 'C')*

When a person holds a rigid and an extreme attitude towards doing the wrong thing, failing to do the right thing or hurting someone's feelings, then they will act or tend to act in a number of ways, the most common of which are as follows:

- They escape from the unhealthy pain of guilt in self-defeating ways (e.g. by using alcohol and drugs to excess).
- They beg forgiveness from the person they have wronged.
- They promise unrealistically that they will not 'sin' again.
- They punish themself physically or by deprivation.
- They defensively disclaim responsibility for wrongdoing.
- They reject offers of forgiveness.
- They hide from people because of their badness.

Such behaviours tend to get in the way of the person thinking clearly about what they did or what they failed to do and the reasons for this. Such thinking is important in that it facilitates understanding and helps the person to learn from the situation.

### 5.3.3.1.4   *Thinking Associated with Guilt (Cognitive 'C')*

When a person holds a rigid and extreme attitude towards doing the wrong thing, failing to do the right thing or hurting someone's feelings, they will tend to think in a number of ways. For example:

- They conclude that, on reflection, they definitely committed the 'sin'.
- They assume more personal responsibility than the situation warrants.
- They assign far less responsibility to others than is warranted.
- They dismiss possible mitigating factors for their behaviour.
- They only see their behaviour in a guilt-related context and fail to put it into an overall context.
- They think that they will receive retribution.
- They think others will shun them because of their badness.
- They ruminate about what they should have done or should not have done and engage in if-only thinking.

As can be seen, such thinking exaggerates the degree of responsibility the person thinks they have, and the negative consequences of their behaviour and also ignores the role of context. Such thinking, again, may be in words or in mental images. As an example of the latter, they may see themself in their mind's eye in a situation where they are taking all the blame for something.

## 5.3.3.2 *Remorse*

The healthy alternative to guilt is remorse.

### 5.3.3.2.1    *The Major Inference Themes in Remorse ('A')*

When a person feels remorse, but not guilt, they make the same inferences at 'A' in the ABC framework as they do when they feel guilt. Namely, they have or think they have:

* *broken their moral code* (i.e. they have done the wrong thing);
* *failed to live up to their moral code* (i.e. they failed to do the right thing);
* *hurt someone's feelings*

### 5.3.3.2.2    *Flexible and Non-extreme Attitudes in Remorse*

When a person feels remorse but not guilt, they hold a flexible attitude and a non-extreme self-acceptance attitude towards one or more of the above inferences.

### 5.3.3.2.3    *Behaviour Associated with Remorse (Behavioural 'C')*

When a person holds a flexible and a non-extreme self-acceptance attitude towards one or more of the above listed inferences and feels remorseful, but not guilty, the following are the most common behaviours associated with remorse.

* They face up to the healthy pain that accompanies the realisation that they have sinned.

- They ask, but do not beg, for forgiveness.
- They understand the reasons for their wrongdoing and act on their understanding.
- They atone for the sin by taking a penalty.
- They make appropriate amends.
- They neither make excuses for their behaviour nor enact other defensive behaviour.
- They do accept offers of forgiveness.
- They face people with their humanity and do not hide from them.

### 5.3.3.2.4   *Thinking Associated with Remorse (Cognitive 'C')*

When a person holds a flexible and a non-extreme self-acceptance attitude towards doing the wrong thing, not doing the right thing or hurting someone's feelings then they will feel remorse, but not guilt and will tend think in a number of ways:

- They take into account all relevant data when judging whether or not they have 'sinned'.
- They assume an appropriate level of personal responsibility.
- They assign an appropriate level of responsibility to others.
- They take into account mitigating factors.
- They put their behaviour into overall context.
- They think that some people may shun them because of what they did or did not do, but most won't do so.
- They think they may be penalised rather than receive retribution.

As the above list shows, the domina
thinking associated with remorse are that it
balanced and that it can be in words or
example of the latter, they may see themself
eye in a situation where they are taking an appropriate level
of responsibility for something, but not all.

## 5.3.4 Shame and Disappointment

In this section, I will consider the ABCs of shame and
disappointment in that order.

### 5.3.4.1 *Shame*

#### 5.3.4.1.1 *The Major Inference Themes in Shame ('A')*

The three major themes in relation to a person's personal
domain that are implicated in shame are:

- *Something highly negative has been revealed about them as a
  person (or about a group with whom they identify) by the
  person themself or by others.*
- *They have acted in a way that falls very short of their ideal.*
- *Others look down on or shun them (or a group with whom
  they identify).*

#### 5.3.4.1.2 *Rigid and Extreme Attitudes in Shame*

In shame the person holds the rigid attitude that they
absolutely should not have revealed the 'shameful'
information, they absolutely should not have fallen very
short of their ideal and that others must not look down on
them. As with guilt the major extreme attitude is a self-
depreciation one and the content of this is some variant of

I'm defective', 'I'm diminished' or 'I'm disgusting', whereas in guilt it is 'I am bad', or 'I am wicked'.

### 5.3.4.1.3  *Behaviour Associated with Shame (Behavioural 'C')*

When a person holds a rigid and an extreme self-depreciation attitude towards a) something highly negative being revealed about them (or a group with whom they identify) by themselves or by others; b) acting in a way that falls very short of their ideal and/or c) others looking down on or shunning them (or a group with whom they identify), then they will act or tend to act in a number of ways, the most common of which are as follows:

- They remove themself from the 'gaze' of others to avoid feeling shame.
- They avoid looking at themself in the mirror to avoid feeling shame.
- They isolate themself from others because they regard themselves as being defective, disgusting or diminished.
- They save face by attacking other(s) who have 'shamed' them.
- They defend their threatened self-esteem in self-defeating ways (e.g. by being excessively defensive and alienating others as a result).
- They ignore attempts by others to restore social equilibrium.

### 5.3.4.1.4  *Thinking Associated with Shame (Cognitive 'C')*

When a person holds a rigid and an extreme self-depreciation attitude towards: (a) something highly negative being revealed about them (or a group with whom they identify) by themselves or by others; (b) acting in a way that falls very short of their ideal; and/or (c) others looking down on or shunning them (or a group with whom they identify), they will tend to think in a number of ways:

- They overestimate the negativity of the information revealed.

- They overestimate the likelihood that the judging group will notice or be interested in the information.

- They overestimate the degree of disapproval they (or their reference group) will receive.

- They overestimate how long any disapproval will last.

- They think that others will shun them because they are defective, disgusting or diminished.

As can be seen, such thinking exaggerates the negative social consequences of the person's behaviour (or that of the member of their identified social group) and also ignores the role of context. As before, such thinking may be in words or in mental images. For example, in the latter, the person may have an image of themselves thinking that others are extraordinarily critical of them for revealing a minor flaw (from an objective standpoint), but which is a major flaw to the person concerned.

### 5.3.4.2 *Disappointment*

The healthy alternative to shame is disappointment.

#### 5.3.4.2.1 *The Major Inference Themes in Disappointment ('A')*

When a person feels disappointment, but not shame, they make the same inferences at 'A' in the ABC framework as they do when they feel shame. Namely, they think that:

- *Something highly negative has been revealed about them (or about a group with whom they identify) by themself or by others.*
- *They have acted in a way that falls very short of their ideal.*
- *Others look down on or shun them (or a group with whom they identify).*

### 5.3.4.2.2  *Flexible    and    Non-extreme    Attitudes    in Disappointment*

When a person feels disappointment, but not shame, they hold a flexible attitude and a non-extreme self-acceptance attitude towards one or more of the above inferences

### 5.3.4.2.3  *Behaviour    Associated    with    Disappointment (Behavioural 'C')*

When a person holds a flexible and a non-extreme self-acceptance attitude towards one or more of the listed inferences and feels disappointment, but not ashamed they act or tend to act in the following ways:

- They continue to participate actively in social interaction.
- They respond positively to attempts of others to restore social equilibrium.

### 5.3.4.2.4  *Thinking    Associated    with    Disappointment (Cognitive 'C')*

When a person holds a flexible and a non-extreme self-acceptance attitude towards one or more of the listed inferences and feels disappointment, but not ashamed they will tend think in a number of ways:

- They see the information revealed in a compassionate self-accepting context.

- They are realistic about the likelihood that the judging group will notice or be interested in the information revealed.

- They are realistic about the degree of disapproval they (or their reference group) will receive.

- They are realistic about how long any disapproval will last.

- They think that while some people might shun them because of what they did or did not do, most won't do so.

As the above list shows, the dominant features of thinking associated with disappointment are that it is realistic and balanced. Please remember again that such thinking may be in words or in mental pictures. As an example of the latter, the person has a mental image of themselves thinking realistically about how much disapproval they will receive having revealed a flaw.

### 5.3.5  Hurt and Sorrow

In this section, I will consider the ABCs of hurt and sorrow in that order.

#### 5.3.5.1 *Hurt*

##### 5.3.5.1.1  *The Major Inference Themes in Hurt ('A')*

The two major themes in relation to a person's personal domain that are implicated in hurt are:

- *Others treat the person badly (and they think they do not deserve such treatment).*
- *Another person has devalued their relationship (i.e. the other indicates that their relationship with the person is less important to them than the relationship is to that person).*

### 5.3.5.1.2   *Rigid and Extreme Attitudes in Hurt*

In hurt, the person holds a rigid attitude and an extreme attitude towards undeserved negative treatment by another or relationship devaluation by that person. While the rigid attitude is at the core of hurt, the extreme attitudes that are derived from the rigid attitude often distinguish between whether the person is experiencing ego 'less me' hurt (where the person depreciates themself) and non-ego 'poor me' hurt (where the person holds an awfulising attitude, finds the adversity intolerable or depreciates life).

### 5.3.5.1.3   *Behaviour Associated with Hurt (Behavioural 'C')*

When a person holds a rigid attitude and an extreme attitude towards undeserved negative treatment by another or relationship devaluation by that person, then they will act or tend to act in a number of ways, the most common of which are as follows:

- The person stops communicating with the other person.
- The person sulks and makes obvious they feel hurt without disclosing details of the matter.
- The person indirectly criticises or punishes the other person for their 'offence'.

### 5.3.5.1.4 *Thinking Associated with Hurt (Cognitive 'C')*

When a person holds a rigid attitude and an extreme attitude towards undeserved negative treatment by another or relationship devaluation by that person, they will tend to think in a number of ways:

- They overestimate the unfairness of the other person's behaviour.
- They think that the other person does not care for them or is indifferent to them.
- They see themself as alone, uncared for or misunderstood.
- They tend to think of past 'hurts'.
- They expect the other to make the first move toward repairing the relationship.

As you can see, such thinking exaggerates the negative consequences of being treated unfairly or having one's relationship devalued by others. Such thinking may yet again be in words or in mental images. An example of the latter is where the person pictures themself all alone in the world, feeling uncared for.

### 5.3.5.2 *Sorrow*

The healthy alternative to hurt is sorrow.

### 5.3.5.2.1 *The Major Inference Themes in Sorrow ('A')*

When a person feels sorrow, but not hurt, they make the same inferences at 'A' in the ABC framework as they do when they feel hurt. Namely, they think that:

- *Others treat the person badly (and they think they do not deserve such treatment).*
- *Another person has devalued their relationship (i.e. the other indicates that their relationship with the person is less important to them than the relationship is to that person).*

### 5.3.5.2.2   *Flexible and Non-extreme Attitudes in Sorrow*

In sorrow, the person holds a flexible attitude and a non-extreme attitude towards undeserved negative treatment by another or relationship devaluation by that person. While the flexible attitude is at the core of sorrow, the non-extreme attitudes that are derived from the flexible attitude often distinguish between whether the person is experiencing self-acceptance sorrow and non-ego sorrow (where the person holds a non-awfulising attitude, finds the adversity tolerable or accepts life, but their view of themselves is not an issue).

### 5.3.5.2.3   *Behaviour Associated with Sorrow (Behavioural 'C')*

When a person holds a flexible attitude and a non-extreme attitude towards one or more of the listed inferences and feels sorrow, but not hurt, they act or tend to act in the following ways:

- They communicate their feelings to the other directly.
- They request, but do not demand, that the other person acts in a fairer manner towards them.

### 5.3.5.2.4   *Thinking Associated with Sorrow (Cognitive 'C')*

When a person holds a flexible attitude and a non-extreme attitude towards one or more of the listed inferences and feels sorrow, but not hurt they will tend think in a number of ways:

- They are realistic about the degree of unfairness in the other person's behaviour.
- They think that the other person has acted badly rather than as demonstrating lack of caring or indifference.
- They see themself as being in a poor situation, but still connected to, cared for by and understood by others not directly involved in the situation.
- If they think of past hurts, they do so with less frequency and less intensity than when they feel hurt.
- They are open to the idea of making the first move towards the other person.

As the above list shows, the dominant features of thinking associated with sorrow are that it is realistic and balanced. Please remember again that such thinking may be in words or in mental pictures. As an example of the latter point, the person has an image of themselves still cared for even though they have been let down.

### 5.3.6   Unhealthy Anger and Healthy Anger[8]

In this section, I will consider the ABCs of unhealthy anger and healthy anger in that order. Please note that both types of anger can be about self, others or life circumstances.

---

[8] Also sometimes referred to as problematic anger vs. non-problematic anger.

### 5.3.6.1 *Unhealthy Anger*

5.3.6.1.1    *The Major Inference Themes in Unhealthy Anger ('A')*

The major themes in relation to a person's personal domain that are implicated in unhealthy anger are:

- *The person has been frustrated in some way.*
- *Their movement towards an important goal has been obstructed in some way.*
- *Someone has transgressed one of their personal rules.*
- *They have transgressed one of their own personal rules.*
- *Someone has shown the person disrespect.*
- *Someone or something has threatened the person's self-esteem.*

5.3.6.1.2    *Rigid and Extreme Attitudes in Unhealthy Anger*

In unhealthy anger, the person holds a rigid attitude and an extreme attitude towards one or more of the inferences listed above. While the rigid belief is at the core of unhealthy anger, the extreme beliefs that are derived from the rigid belief often distinguish between whether the person is experiencing ego unhealthy anger (where the person depreciates themself) and non-ego unhealthy anger (where the person holds an awfulising attitude or finds the adversity intolerable). The person may, of course, experience both unhealthy ego anger unhealthy anger and unhealthy non-ego anger in a given situation. Here the person is unhealthily anger towards another person both because that person has disrespected them and they feel badly about themselves and because the other person has broken one of their rules. In both these situations rigid attitudes lie at the base of the person's unhealthy anger.

5.3.6.1.3 *Behaviour Associated with Unhealthy Anger (Behavioural 'C')*

When a person holds a rigid attitude and an extreme attitude towards the inferences listed above, then they will act or tend to act in a number of ways, the most common of which are as follows:

- They attack the other(s) physically.
- They attack the other(s) verbally.
- They attack the other(s) passive-aggressively.
- They displace the attack on to another person, animal or object.
- They withdraw aggressively.
- They recruit allies against the other(s).

It can be seen from the above list that the main purpose of most of these behaviours (and action tendencies) is to destroy or avoid the other whom the person thinks (albeit wrongly) has made them angry. However, such destructive or avoidance behaviour is largely responsible for the maintenance of unhealthy anger since it prevents the person from facing up to the situation in which they make themself unhealthily angry and from dealing with the issues involved in a healthy manner.

5.3.6.1.4 *Thinking Associated with Unhealthy Anger (Cognitive 'C')*

When a person holds a rigid attitude and an extreme attitude towards the inferences listed above, they will tend to think in a number of ways:

- They overestimate the extent to which the other(s) acted deliberately.
- They see malicious intent in the motives of the other(s).
- They see themself as definitely right and the other(s) as definitely wrong.
- They are unable to see the point of view of the other(s).
- They plot to exact revenge.
- They ruminate about the other's behaviour and imagine coming out on top.

It is important to note that such thinking in unhealthy anger may be in words or in mental images. As an example of the latter, the person sees themselves hurting the other person as an act of revenge for an ego insult.

### 5.3.6.2 *Healthy Anger*

The healthy alternative to unhealthy anger is healthy anger.

#### 5.3.6.2.1   *The Major Inference Themes in Healthy Anger ('A')*

When a person feels healthy anger they make the same inferences at 'A' in the ABC framework as they do when they unhealthy anger (i.e. *frustration, transgression and ego insult*).

#### 5.3.6.2.2   *Flexible and Non-extreme Attitudes in Healthy Anger*

In healthy anger, the person holds a flexible attitude and a non-extreme attitude towards being frustrated, rule transgression, being disrespected etc. While the flexible attitude is at the core of healthy anger, the non-extreme attitudes that are derived from the flexible attitude often distinguish between whether the person is experiencing self-acceptance-based healthy anger and non-ego healthy anger (where the person holds a non-awfulising attitude, finds the adversity tolerable or accepts the other or life conditions).

### 5.3.6.2.3 *Behaviour Associated with Healthy Anger (Behavioural 'C')*

When a person holds a flexible attitude and a non-extreme attitude towards one or more of the listed inferences and feels healthy rather than unhealthy anger, they act or tend to act in the following ways:

- They assert themself with the other(s).
- They request, but do not demand, behavioural change from the other(s).
- They leave an unsatisfactory situation non-aggressively after taking steps to deal with it.

### 5.3.6.2.4 *Thinking Associated with Healthy Anger (Cognitive 'C')*

When a person holds a flexible attitude and a non-extreme attitude towards one or more of the listed inferences and feels healthy rather than unhealthy anger, they will tend think in a number of ways:

- They think that the other(s) may have acted deliberately, but they also recognise that this may not have been the case.
- They are able to see the point of view of the other(s).
- They have fleeting, rather than sustained thoughts to exact revenge or none at all.
- They think that other(s) may have had malicious intent in their motives, but they also recognise that this may not have been the case.

- They think that they are probably rather than definitely right and the other(s) are probably rather than definitely wrong.

As the above list shows, the dominant features of thinking associated with healthy anger are that it is realistic and balanced. Please remember again that such thinking may be in words or in mental pictures. As an example of the latter the person may have an image of them asserting themselves with the person who has insulted their ego.

### 5.3.7   Unhealthy Jealousy and Healthy Jealousy[9]

In this section, I will consider the ABCs of unhealthy jealousy and healthy jealousy in that order.

#### 5.3.7.1 *Unhealthy Jealousy*

While a person may experience unhealthy jealousy in relationships that are not romantic in nature, in this section I will focus on unhealthy jealousy within the context of romantic relationships since (a) it is the most common form of jealousy and (b) it brings out quite vividly how someone's mind works in this emotional problem.

##### 5.3.7.1.1    *The Major Inference Themes in Unhealthy Jealousy ('A')*

The major themes in relation to a person's personal domain that are implicated in unhealthy jealousy are:

---

[9] Also sometimes referred to as problematic jealousy vs. non-problematic jealousy

- *A threat is posed to a person's relationship with their partner from a third person.*

- *A threat is posed by the uncertainty the person faces concerning their partner's whereabouts, behaviour, thoughts and feelings in the context of the first threat.*

### 5.3.7.1.2    *Rigid and Extreme Attitudes in Unhealthy Jealousy*

In unhealthy jealousy, the person holds a rigid attitude and an extreme attitude towards one or both of the inferences listed above. While the rigid belief is at the core of unhealthy jealousy, the extreme beliefs that are derived from the rigid belief often distinguish between whether the person is experiencing ego unhealthy jealousy (where the person depreciates themself) and non-ego unhealthy anger (where the person holds an awfulising attitude towards uncertainty, finds such uncertainty intolerable or depreciates their partner and/or rival). The person may, of course, experience both unhealthy ego jealousy and unhealthy non-ego jealousy in a given situation.

### 5.3.7.1.3    *Behaviour Associated with Unhealthy Jealousy (Behavioural 'C')*

When a person holds a rigid attitude and an extreme attitude towards one or both of the two threats listed above, then they will act or tend to act in a number of ways, the most common of which are as follows:

- They seek constant reassurance that they are loved.

- They monitor the actions and feelings of their partner.

- They search for evidence that their partner is involved with someone else.

- They attempt to restrict the movements or activities of their partner.
- They set tests which their partner has to pass.
- They retaliate for their partner's presumed infidelity.
- They sulk.

### 5.3.7.1.4 *Thinking Associated with Unhealthy Jealousy (Cognitive 'C')*

When a person holds a rigid attitude and an extreme attitude towards a threat that they think is posed by someone else to their relationship and they face uncertainty concerning their partner's whereabouts, behaviour or thinking, then they will tend to think in a number of ways:

- They exaggerate any threat that does exist to their relationship.
- They think the loss of their relationship is imminent.
- They misconstrue their partner's ordinary conversations with relevant others as having romantic or sexual connotations.
- They construct visual images of their partner's infidelity.
- If their partner admits to finding another person attractive, they think that s/he finds that person more attractive than them and that s/he will leave them for this other person.

As you can see, such thinking exaggerates the negative consequences of the perceived threat to your relationship. Such thinking may be in words or in mental images. As an example of the latter, the person pictures in their mind's eye their partner flirting sexually with an attractive member of the opposite sex.

### 5.3.7.2 *Healthy Jealousy*

The healthy alternative to unhealthy jealousy is healthy jealousy. Healthy jealousy is a concept that is foreign to a lot of people and thus, it is important that people use terms that are more acceptable to them (e.g. concern for their relationship).

#### 5.3.7.2.1 *The Major Inference Theme in Healthy Jealousy ('A')*

When a person feels healthy jealousy they make the same inferences at 'A' in the ABC framework as they do when they experience unhealthy jealousy.

- *A threat is posed to a person's relationship with their partner from a third person.*

- *A threat is posed by the uncertainty the person faces concerning their partner's whereabouts, behaviour, thoughts and feelings in the context of the first threat.*

#### 5.3.7.2.2 *Flexible and Non-extreme Attitudes in Healthy Jealousy*

In healthy jealousy, the person holds a flexible attitude and a non-extreme attitude towards relationship threats and relationship-related uncertainty threats. While the flexible attitude is at the core of healthy jealousy the non-extreme attitudes that are derived from the flexible attitude often distinguish between whether the person is experiencing self-acceptance-based healthy jealousy and non-ego healthy jealousy (where the person holds a non-awfulising attitude, finds the relationship-threatening adversity tolerable or accepts the other(s) or life conditions).

### 5.3.7.2.3 *Behaviour Associated with Healthy Jealousy (Behavioural 'C')*

When a person holds a flexible attitude and a non-extreme attitude towards relationship threats and relationship-related uncertainty threats and feels healthy rather than unhealthy jealousy, they act or tend to act in the following ways:

- They allow their partner to initiate expressing love for them without prompting her/him or seeking reassurance once s/he has done so.
- They allow their partner freedom without monitoring his/her feelings, actions and whereabouts.
- They allow their partner to show natural interest in members of the opposite sex without setting tests.
- Due to their concern they strive to treat their partner in ways that are in keeping with their close trusting bond with their partner.

### 5.3.7.2.4 *Thinking Associated with Healthy Jealousy (Cognitive 'C')*

When a person holds a flexible attitude and a non-extreme attitude towards relationship threats and relationship-related uncertainty threats and feels healthy rather than unhealthy jealousy as a result, they will tend think in a number of ways:

- They tend not to exaggerate any threat to their relationship that does exist.

- They do not misconstrue ordinary conversations between their partner and another men/women.
- They do not construct visual images of their partner's presumed infidelity.
- They accept that their partner will find others attractive but they do not see this as a threat.

As the above list shows, the dominant features of thinking associated with healthy jealousy are that it is realistic and balanced. Please remember again that such thinking may be in words or in mental pictures. As an example of the latter they may have an image of their partner chatting in a non-threatening way to an attractive member of the opposite sex.

### 5.3.8    Unhealthy Envy and Healthy Envy[10]

In this section, I will consider the ABCs of unhealthy envy and healthy envy in that order.

#### 5.3.8.1 *Unhealthy Envy*

##### 5.3.8.1.1    *The Major Inference Theme in Unhealthy Envy ('A')*

The major theme in relation to a person's personal domain that is implicated in unhealthy envy is: *someone has something that the person prizes, but does not have.* In unhealthy envy the person's focus may be on the object,[11] i.e. they think they really want the object, whether or not they do (I call this

---

[10] Also sometimes referred to as problematic envy vs. non-problematic envy

[11] I am using the word 'object' here very broadly to include anything that you prize.

object-focused unhealthy envy) or on the person who has the object i.e. the person only prizes the object because the particular person has it (I call this person-focused unhealthy envy). The common denominator in these different types of envy is that the person considers themself to be in a state of deprivation.

### 5.3.8.1.2   *Rigid and Extreme Attitudes in Unhealthy Envy*

In unhealthy envy, the person holds a rigid attitude and an extreme attitude towards someone having something that the person prizes, but does not have. While the rigid belief is at the core of unhealthy envy, the extreme beliefs that are derived from the rigid belief often distinguish between whether the person is experiencing ego unhealthy envy (where the person depreciates themself for not having the desired object) and non-ego unhealthy envy (where the person holds an awfulising attitude towards not having the desired object or finds the deprivation of the desired object intolerable). The person may, of course, experience both unhealthy ego envy and unhealthy non-ego envy in a given situation.

### 5.3.8.1.3   *Behaviour Associated with Unhealthy Envy (Behavioural 'C')*

When a person holds a rigid attitude and an extreme attitude towards someone having something that the person desires but does have, then they will act or tend to act in a number of ways, the most common of which are as follows:

- They disparage verbally the person who has the desired possession to others.
- They disparage verbally the desired possession to others.

- If they had the chance they might take away the desired possession from the other (either so that they will have it or that the other is deprived of it).

- If they had the chance they might spoil or destroy the desired possession so that the other person does not have it.

### 5.3.8.1.4 *Thinking Associated with Unhealthy Envy (Cognitive 'C')*

When a person holds a rigid attitude and an extreme attitude towards someone having something that the person desires but does have, then they will tend to think in a number of ways:

- They tend to denigrate in their mind the value of the desired possession and/or the person who possesses it.

- They may try to convince themself that they are happy with their possessions (although they are not).

- They think about how to acquire the desired possession regardless of its usefulness.

- They think about how to deprive the other person of the desired possession.

- They think about how to spoil or destroy the other's desired possession.

It is important to note that such thinking in unhealthy envy may be in words or in mental images. As an example, the person pictures themselves spoiling the object for the other person.

**5.3.8.2 *Healthy Envy***

The healthy alternative to unhealthy envy is healthy envy.

### 5.3.8.2.1   *The Major Inference Theme in Healthy Envy ('A')*

When a person feels healthy envy they make the same inference at 'A' in the ABC framework as they do when they feel unhealthy envy, i.e. *someone has something that the person prizes, but does not have.*

### 5.3.8.2.2   *Flexible and Non-extreme Attitudes in Healthy Envy*

In healthy envy, the person holds a flexible attitude and a non-extreme attitude towards someone having something that they prize but do not have. While the flexible attitude is at the core of healthy envy the non-extreme attitudes that are derived from the flexible attitude often distinguish between whether the person is experiencing self-acceptance-based healthy envy and non-ego healthy envy (where the person holds a non-awfulising attitude, finds the adversity tolerable or accepts the other or life conditions).

### 5.3.8.2.3   *Behaviour Associated with Healthy Envy (Behavioural 'C')*

When a person holds a flexible attitude and a non-extreme attitude towards someone having something that the person prizes, but does not have and feels healthy rather than unhealthy envy, they will act or tend to act in the following ways:

- They strive to obtain the desired possession if it is truly what they want act.

- They may attempt to model the other person's behaviour to get the desired possession if it is truly what they want.

- They ask help from the person who has the desired possession so that they can get it, if it is truly what they want.

- They cultivate the skill or other quality that they see the other possesses and which they admire.

### 5.3.8.2.4   *Thinking Associated with Healthy Envy (Cognitive 'C')*

When a person holds a flexible attitude and a non-extreme attitude towards one or more of the listed inferences and feels healthy rather than unhealthy envy, they will tend think in a number of ways:

- They honestly admit to themself that they desire the desired possession.

- They are honest with themself if they are not happy with their possessions, rather than defensively trying to convince themself that they are happy with them when they are not.

- They think about how to obtain the desired possession because they desire it for healthy reasons.

- They can allow the other person to have and enjoy the desired possession without denigrating that person or the possession.

As the above list shows, the dominant features of thinking associated with healthy envy are that it is realistic and balanced. Please remember again that such thinking may be in words or in mental pictures. As an example of the latter, the person imagines how they are going to get the desired object having first been clear with themselves that they really want it.

### 5.3.9 Other Consequences of Rigid and Extreme Attitudes and Flexible and Non-extreme Attitudes

So far in this chapter, I have looked at the disturbed consequences of holding rigid and extreme attitudes towards a range of adversities and contrasted these with the more healthy consequences of holding flexible and non-extreme attitudes towards those same adversities. I showed the full range of emotional problems that people experience when they hold rigid and extreme attitudes and the alternatives to these problems when they hold flexible and non-extreme attitudes.

In addition to these emotional problems and healthy alternatives, rigid and extreme attitudes help explain a range of problems that are more behavioural in nature, but which are linked to these emotional problems. Thus, rigid and extreme attitudes tend to underpin a range of self-discipline problems (including procrastination) and problems of addiction.

#### 5.3.9.1 *Procrastination as an Example*

Let me take procrastination as an example here (Dryden, 2012). People often hold a range of rigid attitudes towards the conditions that they consider must exist before they begin a task that they have been procrastinating over (e.g. comfort, confidence, a sense of competence, a sense of motivation, being in the mood, understanding the material immediately, pressure and immediate gratification). The result is continued procrastination, particularly if these demands are accompanied by a philosophy of discomfort intolerance.

Instead, if they hold a set of flexible attitudes towards the aforementioned conditions and regard such conditions as desirable rather than necessary and acknowledge that it is possible for them to begin an activity in the absence of such desired conditions, then they are much more likely to begin these avoided activities and deal effectively with their problem with procrastination. This is particularly the case if they implement a discomfort tolerance philosophy, where they show themselves that tolerating the discomfort of doing something under unfavourable conditions is (a) difficult, (b) possible to do and (c) in their interest to do. In addition, they need to (d) assert their willingness to endure such discomfort and, finally (e) commit themselves to do so behaviourally.

I hope that I have shown in this chapter the crucial role that attitudes play in REBT and how they make a difference to how people can handle life's adversities

# 6

# Summary

Let me summarise what I have done in this book.

I began by briefly explaining what Rational Emotive Behaviour Therapy (REBT) is.

Then, I went on to suggest that the term 'attitude' replace the term 'belief' as the mediating variable between the adversities that we face and our responses to these adversities

Next, I outlined the core components of rigid and extreme attitudes and of flexible non-extreme attitudes and outlined their respective characteristics.

Finally, I detailed the consequences of holding both sets of attitudes in the face of a variety of adversities.

I hope that you found this book useful and welcome your feedback on this book c/o windy@windydryden.com or info@rationalitypublications.com.

# References

Beck, A.T. (1976). *Cognitive Therapy and the Emotional Disorders.* New York: International Universities Press.

Beck, A.T., Epstein, N. & Harrison, R. (1983). Cognitions, attitudes and personality dimensions in depression. *British Journal of Cognitive Psychotherapy,* 1(1): 1–16.

Colman, A. (2015). *Oxford Dictionary of Psychology.* 4th edn. Oxford: Oxford University Press.

David, D. (2015). Rational emotive behavior therapy. In R. L. Cautin & S.O. Lilienfeld (eds), *Encyclopedia of Clinical Psychology.* Hoboken, NJ: Wiley-Blackwell.

David, D., Szentagotai, A., Lupu, V. & Cosman, D. (2008). Rational emotive behavior therapy, cognitive therapy, and medication in the treatment of major depressive disorder: A randomized clinical trial, post-treatment outcomes, and six-month follow-up. *Journal of Clinical Psychology,* 64: 728–46.

Dryden, W. (1999). Beyond LFT and discomfort disturbance: The case for the term 'non-ego disturbance'. *Journal of Rational-Emotive & Cognitive-Behavior Therapy,* 17(3): 165–200.

Dryden, W. (2009). *Skills in Rational Emotive Behaviour Counselling and Psychotherapy.* London: Sage.

Dryden, W. (2012). Dealing with procrastination: The REBT approach and a demonstration session. *Journal of Rational-Emotive & Cognitive-Behavior Therapy,* 30, 264–81.

Dryden, W. (2013). *The ABCs of REBT: Perspectives on Conceptualization.* New York: Springer.

Dryden, W., Beal, D., Jones, J. & Trower, P. (2010). The REBT competency scale for clinical and research applications. *Journal of Rational-Emotive & Cognitive-Behavior Therapy,* 28 (4): 165–216.

Dryden, W., David, D. & Ellis, A. (2010). Rational emotive behavior therapy. In K.S. Dobson (ed.), *Handbook of Cognitive-behavioral Therapies,* 3rd edn, pp. 226–76. New York: Guilford.

Dryden, W., Gordon, J., & Neenan, M. (1997). *What Is Rational Emotive Behaviour Therapy? A Personal and Practical Guide.* Loughton, Essex: Gale Centre Publications.

Eagly, A.H. & Chaiken, S. (1993). *The Psychology of Attitudes.* Harcourt Brace Jovanovich College Publishers.

Ellis, A. (1959). Requisite conditions for basic personality change. *Journal of Consulting Psychology,* 23: 538–40.

Ellis, A. ([1962]1994). *Reason and Emotion in Psychotherapy. Revised and Updated.* New York: Birch Lane Press.

Ellis, A. (1979). Discomfort anxiety: A new cognitive-behavioral construct (Part I). *Rational Living,* 14(2): 3–8.

Ellis, A. (1980). Discomfort anxiety: A new cognitive-behavioral construct (Part II). *Rational Living,* 15(1): 25–30.

Ellis, A. (2004). Why rational emotive behavior therapy is the most comprehensive and effective form of behavior therapy. *Journal of Rational-Emotive & Cognitive-Behavior Therapy,* 22: 85–92.

Ellis, A. & Joffe Ellis, D. (2011). *Rational Emotive Behavior Therapy.* Washington, DC: American Psychological Association.

Engels, G.I., Garnefsky, N. & Diekstra, F.W. (1993). Efficacy of rational-emotive therapy: A quantitative analysis. *Journal of Consulting & Clinical Psychology, 61,* 1083–90.

Harvey, A., Watkins, E., Mansell, W. & Shafran, R. (2004). *Cognitive Behavioural Processes across Psychological Disorders: A Transdiagnostic Approach to Research and Treatment.* Oxford, UK: Oxford University Press.

Hauck, P.A. (1973). *Overcoming Depression.* Philadelphia, PA: Westminster Press.

Hayes, S.C., Strosahl, K.D. & Wilson, K.G. (1999). *Acceptance and Commitment Therapy: An Experiential Approach to Behavior Change.* New York: Guilford Press.

Hogg, M. & Vaughan, G. (2005). *Social Psychology,* 4th edn. London: Prentice-Hall.

Lyons, L.C. & Woods, P.J. (1991). The efficacy of rational-emotive therapy: A quantitative review of the outcome research. *Clinical Psychology Review,* 11: 357–69.

Vîslă, A., Flückiger, C., grosse Holtforth, M. & David, D. (2016). Irrational beliefs and psychological distress: A meta-analysis. *Psychotherapy and Psychosomatics,* 85: 8–15.

Wills, F. (2009). *Beck's Cognitive Therapy: Distinctive Features.* Hove, East Sussex: Routledge.

# Index

117